'TIL THE ROAD YOU TROD

ENHANCING LAW ENFORCEMENT IN THE BAHAMAS

WELBOURNE BOOTLE

Copyrights

'Til the Road You Trod: Enhancing Law Enforcement In The Bahamas © 2024 by Welbourne Bootle. All rights reserved.

ISBN 9798305898712

Welbourne Bootle
P. O. Box F-41417,
Freeport, Grand Bahama,
Bahamas

Inspire Publishing (Bahamas)
P. O. Box CB-11990
Nassau, Bahamas
www.InspirePublishing.org

No portion of this book may be reproduced for sale or distribution in any form without written permission from the author.

DEDICATION

This book is dedicated to my wonderful wife, Melrose. You are a constant source of inspiration, urging me to keep moving forward, pushing my limits, and striving for more. Thank you for encouraging me to share my journey. Writing this book was such a delightful experience; it rekindled so many cherished memories. I am truly grateful for your steadfast support and love.

The Bootle Family

ACKNOWLEDGMENTS

I want to express my heartfelt appreciation for my children. Each of you are brilliant in your unique way, teaching me something new every day. I admire your independence and commitment to everything you pursue. With the grace of God, you will achieve even more. Keep moving forward; your journey is unfolding!

My journey is committed to my grandchildren. They have brought me so much joy. Meeting the next generation is a special gift from God. Their inquiring minds have baffled me and their knowledge is far beyond my comprehension. Prayerfully, I will welcome more to this clan by the grace of God. Valiyah, Tré, Gabriel Camayel, Elijah, Kadens, Dejà, Olivia, Malik, D'Shae, Zion, Wes, David, et al., get to know your true identity, search your past, and piece together what will direct your future. Love, G.D.!

I'd also like to thank the following persons for their contributions, especially Everett "Bulla" Bootle for his invaluable information and sharp memory. I thank Albert "Abba" Bootle, Captian Elmore "Forty" Sawyer, Wellington Francis, Lyndy Knowles, Keith Mason, Irvin "Dopy" Taylor, Tyrone "Rock" Morris, Romardo Cash, President Grand Bahama Dock & Allied Workers Union (GBDAWU), and Obie Ferguson Jr., KC, President Commonwealth of the Bahamas Trade Union Congress (CBTUC), "C" Squad 1972/73 RBPF.

FOREWORD

As The Commonwealth of The Bahamas is ushered into celebrating 52 years of independence, it is paramount that more Bahamians capture our history and culture by documenting their experiences, gratuitously sharing their insights, and unapologetically dispensing their counsel regarding the multifaceted elements necessary to make this country the best it's ever been. Welbourne Bootle, in delivering this noble work to us, has done just that: poured his head, heart, and soul into a literary work that is no less than a treasure to our nation.

A son of the soil and, more specifically, an "Abaco Boy," Bootle takes us on a journey that encapsulates both his personal challenges and triumphs and the professional landmarks that have shaped him as both a man and a lawman.

His is a unique perspective on nation crafting and building, having been a member of that distinguished squad who served up front and center on the evening of July 9, 1973, when the Union Jack was lowered over our islands for the last time and gloriously replaced by our foremost symbol of social freedom and togetherness: the aquamarine, gold and black flag of The Commonwealth of The Bahamas.

The Royal Bahamas Police Force, in particular, and law enforcement in general, own such a rich history in our nation, and Bootle has appropriately infused this historical account with the humanness of his own experiences and life lessons in a style that is easy to read and pleasant to digest. One can hear his national pride ringing through as he addresses some of the complexities of policing in an archipelago and offers solutions, not just for the Family Islands as a collective but for specific islands with distinguishable needs.

I commend my comrade for offering up a portion on recruitment. Indeed, those of us who served on the Royal Bahamas Police Force are, for the most part, a happy band who remember well what an honourable thing it was to have been recruited to this noble profession. Furthermore, Bootle has examined the situations that sponsor much concern for our people, and has courageously suggested that recruitment begin as early as primary school since it is never too early to instill a respect for the law, for order, and for responsible citizenry.

You do yourself a service to read this notable rendition of Bootle's Bahamas, for even as this nation belongs to all of us, it belongs to each of us, and Bootle has done his just dessert in presenting with integrity and celebration his career and his country while encouraging us to position ourselves aright so that indeed "the road we trod may lead unto our God."

Well done Welbourne Bootle, well done! If islands could salute, Abaco would salute you. Then again, through you, Abaco has made a remarkable contribution to this extraordinary nation and on behalf of my fellow countrymen, I give you thanks.

Wellington M. Francis
Former Deputy Superintendent of Police
Royal Bahamas Police Force

Table of Contents

DEDICATION i
ACKNOWLEDGMENTS iii
FOREWORD v
INTRODUCTION 1

Chapter 1
   TRAGEDY 7

Chapter 2
   PARENTS AND SIBLINGS 15

Chapter 3
   LIFE'S LESSONS: PREPARING THE FUTURE
   GENERATION 19

Chapter 4
   BECOMING: INQUIRING MIND 23

Chapter 5
   PREPARATION FOR GLOBAL CHALLENGES 27

Chapter 6
   POLITICS 29

Chapter 7
   THE ROAD TO INDEPENDENCE 35

Chapter 8
   JULY 10, 1973 43

Chapter 9
   TRAINING 53

Chapter 10
   SPECIAL UNIT MISSIONS 61

Chapter 11
   RECOMMENDATIONS 75

Chapter 12
   FINAL THOUGHTS 85

'TIL THE ROAD YOU TROD

ENHANCING LAW ENFORCEMENT IN THE BAHAMAS

> "The fight for justice against corruption is never easy. It never has been and it never will be. It exacts a toll on our self, our families, our friends, and especially our children. In the end, I believe, as in my case, the price we pay is well worth holding on to our dignity."
>
> *Frank Serpico*

INTRODUCTION

I found myself reflecting on the coronation of the new king of England coinciding with The Bahamas' fiftieth anniversary of Independence. As I watched the ceremonies and observed the emotions of the British people, it reminded me of the night the Union Jack was lowered for the last time in our country, making way for our new Bahamian flag—marking the birth of an independent nation. I was a Bahamian. Can you believe it? To be a Bahamian meant no longer being a British subject. I had the privilege to experience these events up close and personal.

From His Royal Highness (HRH) Prince Charles to HRH King Charles III was a long journey filled with fanfare and drama. When we received him fifty years ago, during that notorious dance with our first lady, Dame Marguerite, Prince Charles was hardly twenty-five years old. For members of my squad in a recently graduated regiment of the Royal Bahamas Police Force, he appeared as our peer, given the way he carried himself. Destined to one day be King of Great Britain, he was oblivious to the realities of life that awaited his learning.

None of us on Prince George Wharf, including him, as he stepped off the HMS Minerva, imagined he would go on to achieve so much charitable good while an understudy to his dear, respected mother. The late Queen Elizabeth II was so endeared and beloved by her country and the Commonwealth. We also could not have imagined that his personal life, filled with intrigue, speculation, and controversy, would be on display for all the world to observe and critique.

In 1973, the young prince visited The Bahamas to give his "assent" to the independence of another former colony seeking its own path. He likely never anticipated that fifty years later, many former colonies would advocate for total secession from Great Britain as fully autonomous republics. Meanwhile, his son, Prince Harry, would transform the monarchy by marrying someone of a different race and nationality, along with publicly revealing some of its secrets.

However, none of these events hindered the crescendo of his destiny—the long and bumpy walk to the kingdom. Fifty years later, just a few weeks ago, through the natural cycle of life, Prince Charles indeed became King Charles. There I was reminiscing over the honored privilege of having been chosen by life and the Royal Bahamas Police Force to be a member of the sacred squad that received and saluted him as he came to, in a roundabout way, deliver the keys of ownership and self-determination to the government and people of the Commonwealth of The Bahamas.

I was there as a young man from Abaco, charting my own new course because of something else I had witnessed. Are our steps truly ordered? Are our fates ultimately guided? Was it a coincidence that I grew up as an inquisitive observer of life who had been moved by the events that saw explosives go off in the harbor near the dock of the island where I had been born and raised, in defiance of the very movement toward independence?

Did something beyond human reason decide long before I was born that I would grow with the personality and disposition that could be so influenced by what I deemed to be insurrection, leading me to join the institution that defends law and order in my country? And then, as if predesigned, at just the right moment in history, I would be in the right place to play a role in the ceremonies marking my country's independence.

As sure as I am convinced about a divine force, and as sure as a prince's journey has led to him becoming king, I am persuaded that my tribute to our country's fiftieth anniversary of independence must serve as a reminder to our people and leaders about a few things.

Firstly, despite our national challenges over the last fifty years, we continue our journey toward successful nationhood, aiming for global acceptance as a developed and fully functional first-world country. We have already made significant progress toward this ambitious goal, especially in infrastructure, technology, and human services. Although we operate with a relatively small national budget and have increasingly taken on debt, we still show a level of stability, even amid external shocks and natural disasters or pandemics. Additionally, we experience a degree of political and civil stability, though some may contend that signs of deterioration are evident.

I believe wholeheartedly that, unlike the journey of Prince Charles to King Charles, our internal struggles and improprieties will not ultimately prevent us from our great destiny.

Secondly, hurricanes—especially Dorian—and a pandemic that caused our country to shut down our number one industry, tourism, have greatly tested us but have proven our resolve. We are without a doubt blessed beyond human effort. Storm after storm has taught us to adapt and even perfect strategies for disaster recovery, especially in Grand Bahama and Abaco. We must find ways to use these experiences to ensure our country's ability to thrive even in the face of the doom of climate change, and even capitalize on sharing this knowledge. And we cannot take for granted our geographical makeup and positioning in the Caribbean. We are profiting right at this moment, with increased visitor numbers because of our proximity to the United States and the visionary ideas of our state-of-the-art deep-water cruise port and international airport on New Providence. We continue to be forerunners in the formula of travel and leisure, notwithstanding our need to diversify our economy.

My career took me to every inhabited island in The Bahamas and many isolated ones by fix-wing aircraft, helicopters, and seacraft. Although Abaco is my favorite one, each island has a unique touch of God's blessings. There is no doubt Exuma and its cays are the most beautiful.

With our determination and divine blessings, it will be our collective effort that fulfills our national aspirations. This is our moment of truth. We must cultivate pride, unity, and a profound sense of patriotism that we pass on to current and future generations, which will secure the next stage of our shared journey. Embracing fundamental values and principles, previously upheld by the common majority for which we fought political and constitutional battles, will shape our destiny. Therefore, the success of our nation rests on the shoulders, hearts, and minds of all capable Bahamians.

Fifty-one years later, we continue to battle within ourselves, extending even beyond the Abaco docks. This conflict infiltrates our homes, schools, public institutions, and the streets, particularly in New Providence. We have become a distracted and misguided society, slightly losing our way due to an insatiable appetite for materialism and individual gain, which comes at the cost of community progress. We still need to learn, like children, how to nourish ourselves, seize control of our economy, and define and achieve Bahamian empowerment. Fifty-one years later, as we commemorate the significant milestone of half a century, we are urged to genuinely recommit to the principles of independence.

And so, I have penned this brief reflection on the last fifty-one years of our journey as a member of the select group of police officers who had the sacred honor of serving on the night we ushered in such a great feat as a little country, as a reminder. I must have been there for a purpose beyond pomp and pageantry. I am alive as a testament to those who don't appreciate our history so that we are not doomed to repeat it. This moment and my part in it must act as an opportunity to whip our leaders back into the actionable calling of our astounding destiny while inspiring a people to take up "arms" again on our divine march to true freedom, 'til the road you've trod lead unto your God ...

We have to march on Bahamaland. And I pray that this brief testimonial, in some small way, encourages us, like a prince who became king and a boy who climbed the ranks of the Royal Bahamas Police Force, to go from strength to strength and glory to glory.

It was regrettable that our squad's involvement in the initial independence ceremonies was overlooked at the fiftieth anniversary celebration. Even after contacting the event's director via email and phone to emphasize the historical importance of our contribution, our chance to participate symbolically and celebrate our collective national pride was not recognized. Although the outcome was disappointing, it does not lessen the pride we take in having served during this historic occasion.

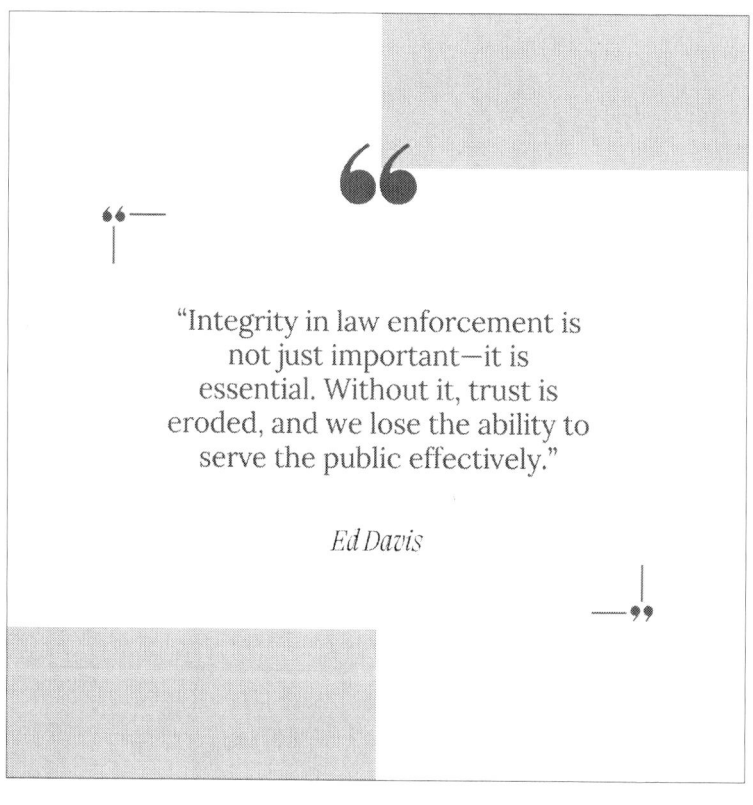

"Integrity in law enforcement is not just important—it is essential. Without it, trust is eroded, and we lose the ability to serve the public effectively."

Ed Davis

Chapter 1
TRAGEDY

Steps—that action of putting one foot in front of the other to reach one's destination. Steps have defined my life and that of my lineage for centuries. But in this instant, I mention the sound of certain indelible steps as the foundation of my formation. At four years old, walking along the shoreline with my best friend and cousin, Wilton Sawyer, I noticed the sound of smaller feet attempting to follow us. I have always been aware of my surroundings and in love with nature. I could detect the rhythm between mine and Wilton's feet maneuvering the rocky shore, even with the presence of the not-too-distant waves and wind. And intuitively, I could feel and hear an interruption of that rhythm by the following of someone smaller.

It was my two-year-old brother, Sidney, trying to catch up with boys twice his age, hoping to tag along and wanting to belong. I turned around not too far from my grandparents' home, recognized him, and motioned for him to go back. I watched him until he was out of sight and seemingly almost back to my grandparents' home. With that, I didn't think anything more of it until later. Wilton and I were up along the shoreline on one of our daily missions north to an area called Big Point.

My heart remains broken to this day as I recall that feeling when Wilton's father, a first cousin, Captain Leonard Sawyer, sounded the community alarm and gathered us children to try to identify the little body he found floating in the water on his way back to our settlement, Cooper's Town, from Ambergris Cay. It was Sidney's little body in a dingy boat, which my eyes saw for myself. I felt responsible. To this day, it bothers me! I truly believe that his spirit is always with me as an angel, always protecting me from the many dangers I have faced. I wondered how the news was received by my mother and father, who were traveling in the United States at the time. They must have been crushed to have lost a child tragically young. I remember crying behind his little homemade coffin as they removed him from our house, heading southeast to the church. My eldest brother Everette, crying, lovingly lifted me up and held me tight, as if to say, "I don't want to lose you too." He took me back home to be with a family member. Even though I was four years old, that scene had a lasting impact on me.

That experience has guided my actions ever since. Grief is seldom completely healed, but if we permit it, we can grow and improve as individuals because of it. Personally, it inspired me to take on a greater sense of responsibility for my younger siblings and the youth in my community, particularly after a momentary lapse in attention led to the tragic loss of my younger brother.

Bootle Value

I was born a Bootle, in Bootle Town, Abaco, more famously known by its adjacent extension, Cooper's Town. It is said that Cooper's Town was named to honor my grandfather's nephew, Branville, the first child born to his sister Dian and her husband, William Cooper. But the people of both townships were all one, no matter the boundaries. The patriarchs of these blended families were my grandfather, Prince Albert Bootle Jr., and my grand uncle, William Cooper.

My grandfather came from Bootle Bay in West End, Grand Bahama a name that honors my family heritage. It is believed that our ancestors were free slaves who emigrated from the Carolinas to Grand Bahama during the Civil War, between 1861 and 1865. He was born in West Grand Bahama in 1875 to Prince Albert Bootle Sr. and Sarah Russell-Bootle. However, by the time my grandfather, the grandson of Pa Musa from West Africa, reached an age of independence, he ventured out on his own. A youthful entrepreneur, he launched sailing points and ventured further east across Grand Bahama, establishing his business between Pineridge, Water Cay, and East Grand Bahama, eventually expanding to Abaco and its Cays, and later to New Providence.

Entrepreneurship was his thing. His further success came from the harvesting and trade of sisal (Agave sisalana)—it's the plant that the rope is made from. Granddad captained his ship in the delivery of sisal successfully for many years, eventually relocating to the area of Abaco now known as Cooper's Town until supply and demand grew to the point where he delivered groceries on his various routes and even passengers to Nassau and Grand Bahama.

Having eventually settled in Bootle Town, Abaco, my grandfather, Prince Albert Bootle Jr., had the foresight to develop a township—bringing in pre-fab and then wooden buildings for the first school and church, ensuring that other settlers had access to education and Christianity. He purchased two buildings from a Canadian gentleman in Hope Town, Elbow Cay. They were used to construct a school and a teacher's residence. His brother Melvin's son, Sherlin C. Bootle, was hired by him as the first schoolteacher. Sherlin C. Bootle's legacy lives on, as the high school in Cooper's Town was named in his honor, along with a portion of the Great Abaco Highway named by the Rt. Hon. Hubert A. Ingraham, MP for the area. As time passed, Prince Albert Jr. was so ingenious that Bootle/Cooper's Town and Fire Road had electricity, privately owned and managed by his eldest son Ronald, assisted by his grandson Joseph Sawyer, along with a private dock and a fuel station, long before much of the Out Islands of The Bahamas received these basic amenities from the government. The extension of electricity to the settlement of Blackwood was the next phase before the

Bahamas Electricity Corporation (BEC) purchased the company.

He later purchased a building from a family in Cedar Harbour, which was used to construct the first church in Cooper's Town. This rich history of a black man achieving so much is interesting for many reasons, but it stands out in its significance to discussions about race and economics. What granddad achieved financially in those times was beyond commendable and demonstrated the potential of blacks with vision if given the freedom to flourish. His life holds lessons for empowerment even in today's reality. Outside of race, it shows that Bahamians can be self-sufficient. We can establish successful communities. We did so in the late 1800s. In the context of race, which was not a defining factor in Abaco at the time, my granddad's example proves that all this talk of black and white is sometimes a distraction because we allow it to be.

I am told so many stories about his philanthropic work; I believe his spirit whispers to me. In my adult life, I ran into an old "Conchy-Joe" gentleman (Caucasian Bahamian) who, when he found out who I was, praised my grandfather, even in death. He told me how kind my granddad was to anyone and everyone he encountered. This gentleman recounted how my grandfather would drop off groceries to the poorest in his community in Abaco and also carry members of his family to New Providence on his boat, free of charge. There was very little segregation in Abaco back then. I mean, because families lived on their own portions of land, our townships looked separate. But we grew up socially integrated—allowing for race talk only as politics became more popular.

My grandfather owned five boats and vessels. He owned the power company until it was sold to the government (BEC) in modern times. He was the owner of a grocery store in Bootle Town and one on Spanish Cay that serviced the Little Abaco settlements and boaters. Granddad also owned a cay and five horses that assisted with the carriage of groceries and other goods. He was a minister of the gospel and, therefore, a faithful, loving family man. And, of course, he was well-traveled and a well-respected national and international businessman. He was asked to look after Spanish Cay, just northwest of Cooper's Town, by its German owner at that time. Several persons were hired to assist on the cay. The cay was later purchased by Sir Oliver Simmonds, a British aviation pioneer and Conservative Party politician. Sir Oliver would hire my grandfather's boat, the "Reaper," to transport locally harvested Solomon's potatoes, barked coconuts, and bananas to New Providence. Sir Oliver graciously allowed him to operate a portion of his business on Spanish Cay.

My uncle, Ronald Bootle, along with first cousins Medious Edgecombe, Fred Edgecombe, Leonard Sawyer, Elvin Sawyer, and other relatives, including Samuel McIntosh Jr., Willis McIntosh, Herbert Pritchard, and Vaney Laing, formed the crew that made several journeys across the Atlantic Ocean to Great Britain on Sir Oliver's luxury yacht. My aunt, Jestina Bootle Russell, was employed by him to oversee the housekeeping department at his newly built Balmoral Beach Hotel in New Providence, which also hosted my wedding reception.

Sir Oliver later sold Spanish Cay to American businessman Clint Murchison, the owner of the NFL football team the Dallas Cowboys at that time. My mother gave me my middle name, Clinton, after Mr. Murchison.

Mr Murchison was a family friend who took a strong interest in my first cousin, Felix Sawyer. Felix shared a very close bond with his two sons and was given a first-class international education, along with opportunities for travel. As young boys, my siblings and I recognized our cousin's uniqueness and looked up to him. He was skillful in water skiing, maneuvering through the waters as the Murchison boat pulled him behind, and cutting through the surface. Later on, he became both a mentor and a close confidant to me. He was flamboyant, articulate, and confident. I looked forward to his returns home from London, England, and I had the pleasure of meeting a few international stars who knew him well at their residences in Paradise Island and New Providence.

Privilege or Austerity

My father's generation, along with his siblings and cousins, were born into privilege. The Bootle narrative isn't one of prejudice or dire poverty, and I'm grateful for that. This isn't boasting. Many Bahamian families across The Bahamas in the post-slavery era, who settled on former plantations and gained ownership of farms, describe a lack of poverty. The late 1800s saw significant wealth gained through hard work and successful businesses, shaping the mindset and values of that generation. It may be unfortunate to acknowledge, but being free from needing welfare or validation from one's country and being born into a sense of equality enables a richer life experience. Conversely, this means there's less pressure to be militant or aggressive, reducing the drive to surpass previous generations.

My father, many of his siblings, and the men in our family were all involved in one of my grandfather's ventures. Unfortunately, since none seemed to have inherited his business savvy, what wasn't wasted, was sold off, leaving little of my grandfather's legacy behind. This is deeply regrettable, as we have possibly forfeited the value and insights stemming from my grandfather's accomplishments. In more developed societies, his life would likely serve as a case study in business for similar communities. Even today, a comprehensive examination of his life could motivate Bahamians in our nation by reminding us that before Franklyn Wilson and the Sunshine Boys, there was a black man in Abaco in the 1800s who achieved significant success. The central message is clear: if it has been accomplished before, it can be achieved again.

Bootle values are timeless and simple. Therefore, we are honest, hardworking, fun-loving people. We do not believe ourselves to be any better or worse than others—rich, poor, white, black, educated, uneducated, and so on. We are grounded in Christian values and have as our foundation a loyalty to community and family because we were born into a combination of both. I believe that we can achieve anything we put our minds to. However, because we are not moved by a strong desire for riches and materialism, it is not a driving force of the present generation. Although several successful businessmen and women remain among us who have achieved great success as entrepreneurs, educators, government workers, civil servants, and in other areas of note.

Grandmother

Grandfather Prince Jr. met my grandmother Eliza in East Grand Bahama. He fell in love with her and decided to take her to Abaco with him, where he had relocated. Soon afterward, they were married. With the help of her sister Margaret, she quietly boarded my grandfather's boat without her parents' knowledge. Mama sailed away with her prince to Abaco, leaving Water Cay and Grand Bahama behind, never to return. She was born on Water Cay, one of thirteen children, and the daughter of Mr. Scipio Baillou, a mega landowner of Old Free Town, Grand Bahama. His registered properties are found in the Registrar General's Office, Commonwealth of The Bahamas. According to his will, my grandmother, the last surviving child, became the sole heir of the estate. The land left to my grandmother includes:

20.5 acres at Burnside Cove
11.5 acres at Tony Maura Point, Gold Rock Creek
8.5 acres at Mangrove Point
120 acres at Sharp Rock

Sharp Rock is a major part of the Carnival Cruise Port Development, now being developed as Celebration Key.

The acquisition of the properties from my grandmother and grand-aunt Margaret Baillou Rolle by another party has been suspicious and left more questions than answers. They were the two surviving siblings at that time. This matter is still a hot topic issue that needs resolution.

Chapter 2
PARENTS AND SIBLINGS

My father, Prince Bootle III, filled his role as his father's son naturally, doing his part in Granddad's empire as a captain of one of his boats, the "CT Mail." But my father truly impressed me as a family man. He and my mother got married young, in 1940, right in Cooper's Town. Together, they had ten children. I am number seven. The first to be born was my brother, Everette.

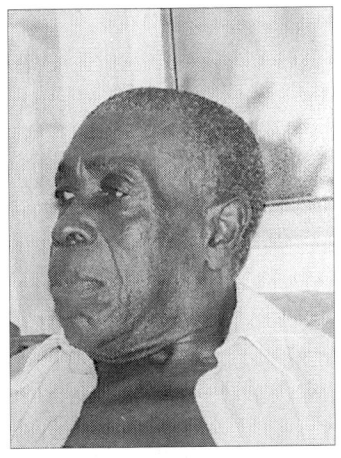
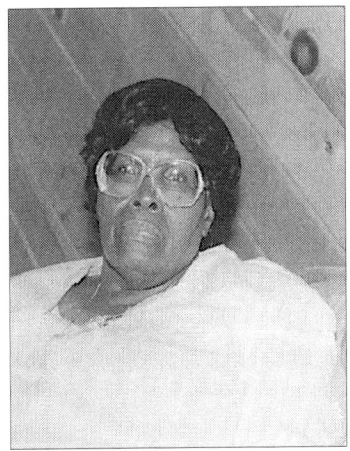

Prince Bootle III   *Isabella Kemp-Bootle*

My mother then birthed four daughters before she had another son: Alice, Ruthmae, Gevena, and Melvern. Next came the very adventurous Albert; he hung out with the older gentlemen in the community. He would sleep in the bow of the small fishing boats just to go on Saturday fishing trips. The boaters wouldn't know he was there until they dropped anchor. We believed he was the favorite of Granddad and our mother. My birth followed his, and then Sidney. Donna was born after Sidney, and then came my baby brother Drexel, whom we called Jackie.

We grew up in a gentle and loving environment. My mother, Isabella Kemp-Bootle, was like an angel. Born to Sylvanus Joseph Kemp of Eleuthera and Alice McIntosh-Kemp of Cooper's Town, she often went from community to community, giving a little something to the less fortunate. I would accompany her most times and paid close attention as she very discreetly slipped money into the hands of so many. She tried not to let anyone see; she was shy and never wanted the spotlight to be on her. She loved politics and, like many women on the Family Islands, went to their graves without recognition of their historical significance in the fight for women's rights to vote. She was the recipient of the prestigious Bahamas National Tourism Achievement Award in 1990.

Mother, however, was best known for her skills in the kitchen. You would expect a son to say that, but this was confirmed by many well-known personalities in The Bahamas. These lucky individuals included Sir Roland Symonette, the first Bahamian premier; Sir Clement Maynard, the second Bahamian deputy prime minister, and other dignitaries, including celebrities like Jimmy Buffett, who visited Treasure Cay frequently. The original owners of Treasure Cay, Dumas Millner and Leonard Thompson, hired her as their personal executive chef. Her food was also often specially packed in sealed containers and exported to places in the United States, Canada, and Europe. Her Bahamian conch chowder was in high demand locally and internationally.

After Treasure Cay was sold to its new owners, over one hundred foreign homeowners hired my mother as their property manager. She used her position in this capacity to secure jobs for native Abaconians and ensured that they were well compensated and respected. She was their "Union." She kept asue for several hundred Treasure Cay employees. Her financial skills and advice were second to none. Mom remained in this unique position until 1994 when she retired and turned her business over to my sister, Donna. She assisted many locals in achieving businesses, homes, and vehicles—something she later reluctantly confided in me.

I learned from my father early how to love and respect a woman. He would be affectionate toward my mother, sometimes throwing his arms around her, proclaiming his love. And she would act kind of shy. But she wasn't too shy when she got angry with him and scolded him for hanging out too late with the boys. Daddy would sit there and just take it quietly. After a while, he would ask her if she was done, very playfully, and then get up and walk away. I asked him one time, "Why do you sit and say nothing when Mother is talking?" He said, "Son, never argue with a woman. Just let them vent because you can't win, whether you are right or wrong." I admired how he would sit through those one-sided arguments, never walking off while Mother was talking. This lesson clearly came back to me as a young rookie. I was detailed to attend to a domestic matter in the Cable Beach area, an upper-class community on New Providence. I was able to speak to the married couple at their residence. Of course, the gentleman was more vocal. He was much bigger than I was. I was alone. Being guided by my parents' example, especially my father's advice, I went to the gentleman and said to him, "You are the prince of this house, sir!" really thinking of my father, whose name was Prince. We had a decent conversation. At the end, he said, "Listen, officer, I am ashamed. You could be our son, and here we are taking simple pointers on life from you, a child."

My dad spent very little time as a school student. However, he was a philosopher. I would be in awe listening to his quick responses to any situation. He would offer philosophical advice and recommendations. He gave me what I recognized as the greatest piece of advice in my life, which guided me through my career. He constantly reminded me, "Son, whatever you do in life, always have sense and be decent!" Simple, but very profound. He instilled this in me over and over again. And that, along with Bootle values and the sad passing of my brother Sidney, is what I believe shaped me into an honest and patriotic son of the soil. Eventually, a police officer serving with distinction.

Chapter 3
LIFE'S LESSONS: PREPARING THE FUTURE GENERATION

Another gentleman who had an impact on my life growing up in Abaco was Mr. Edmond Spencer Moxey. In the 1960s, he worked as a wireless operator in Cooper's Town for the Bahamas Telecommunication Company. He would voluntarily help the young men in the community, educating them. Whether socializing, discussing politics, music, or any positive topic, he particularly focused on grooming young men to be gentlemen and respect ladies. I always enjoyed his skills on the accordion; he was truly a master of his musical abilities. He was a fixture at our home. My mother always ensured that his meals were prepared and ready for him. He spoke at my wedding on behalf of my mother and expressed his gratitude for her accepting him as a son in a strange place away from his family. Mr. Moxey was very excited when he found out I played the keyboard. We never had the chance to have that musical session together. I know that my love for the keyboard grew from witnessing this musical genius. The Honorable Edmund Spencer Moxey went on to become a member of parliament and a political and cultural icon in The Bahamas, the mastermind behind one of the most significant cultural centers in the history of our country to date: Jumbey Village.

False Accusations

I recalled an incident at Treasure Cay, Abaco. I was about thirteen years old, with my cousin Kenneth Murray Jr., whom we affectionately called "Cody." He was seven months older than I. After school, we would usually find ourselves moving around Cooper's Town, Fire Road, or Treasure Cay. This particular evening, we stopped at a gentleman's living accommodation in Treasure Cay. We never went inside his home; we saw him and decided to stop and chat with him. Later that evening, our fathers summoned us. We were questioned about a missing wallet that the same gentleman we had visited earlier was now accusing us of stealing. He was accompanied by Immigration Officer William Billie Nottage, now a Bahamian diplomat; I guess because there were no police officers posted in Treasure Cay at the time. I knew that we were innocent. Therefore, I had no fear, but I was very concerned. I assured my father of this. Uncle Kenneth Sr. was told the same thing by Ken Jr.

At the gentleman's living quarters, he unlocked the door and invited us in, saying that we were the only people in his room. He pointed out to our fathers and Officer Nottage where he changed his clothes. As he lifted his pants, his wallet dropped to the ground. Needless to say, our fathers had some unsophisticated choice words for him that I care not to repeat. They admonished him never to accuse us of such a heinous act again. We felt immense pride and excitement knowing our fathers defended us, reflecting their confidence in us as young men. Ken Jr. went on to become a very successful businessman in New Providence, the owner of Murray's Souse House, arguably the best-tasting souse in the whole country.

This incident helped me tremendously in my career. We must listen to everyone accused of committing a crime. This is why proper and effective investigations are so important. Anytime an innocent person goes to prison, the investigator has failed. Obviously, society is robbed of a potential productive member citizen. A simple lesson in investigation is, "Every contact leaves a trace." It is there; find it!

I saw the gentleman in Freeport many years later and thanked him for that incident. I believed it gave me a ministry. While serving, I looked at accused persons who had been arrested, and with this in mind, I went all out as a crime scene forensic specialist to ensure that the evidence presented was collected and analyzed methodically to prove innocence or guilt—no in-between.

Changing Mindset

I was deeply interested in understanding why some young people would opt for crime and prison instead of pursuing honest work and freedom. I took the initiative to engage in one-on-one discussions and sometimes spoke with groups of incarcerated young men. Most of my conversations took place at the Internal Security Division (ISD) of the Royal Bahamas Police Force (RBPF). Each person shared fascinating stories and many genuinely sought a better path forward. While a few maintained their innocence, I encouraged them to consider a more positive future. Given their youth, they possess so much potential to contribute positively to society. I firmly believe we need to find ways to engage our youth. Otherwise, we risk perpetuating the cycle of recidivism, as prison is increasingly becoming a revolving door and crime rates are soaring uncontrollably.

Some time ago, I went to Nassau from Freeport to attend the Supreme Court while serving on Grand Bahama. I was stopped by a young man on Bay Street who was calling out my name. He asked if I remembered him. I did not. He told me that he was a prison inmate on a work assignment at the Internal Security Division, RBPF, where I worked at the time. He reminded me that I had talked with them, advising them to do something different with their lives and encouraging them. He said that he remembered the talks I had with them and that he had turned his life around. He told me that he was now a businessman, located in the downtown area of Nassau. It was a good feeling, knowing that a young man was seeking a better way of life.

Chapter 4
BECOMING: INQUIRING MIND

There's a revolution coming in the educational system worldwide. It's called regenerative learning. A colleague has introduced me to the concept. If you log onto www.designed4resilience.org, you can learn more about it. It asks two very important questions on the site. 1. "What if young people found meaningful, healing purpose and connected with nature and other people to co-create just and abundant worlds?" 2. "How might we tap into the gifts nature has given us to co-create lives full of love, justice, and abundance beyond our future phobia?"

While this development in education is happening in response to climate change and natural disasters, I can say that this was the way I learned back in the 1950s and '60s as a boy. Born in 1954, I came here a little strange—a little more curious than the other children in my home and community. I always had a connection with nature, so much so that from my earliest school days, my parents sent me out to school a little earlier than the others, and I still got there late. Often, I arrived just after the first period, and my teachers just got used to it. Thanks to my older brother Albert, he would sometimes hold my hand to help me get to school on time. I knew this frustrated him sometimes because I always wanted to see what was cracking in the bushes.

On the way to school, I tended to walk along the shoreline to see and monitor the ocean, take in the breeze, and observe the creatures in the rocks at the shoreline. Between the shoreline and the cement road stood a bushy area that provided a little shade and cover from being seen, but was also home to many small animals, reptiles, birds, and insects. These living things, along with the trees and shrubbery, were my real learning tools. I was particularly fascinated by the various types of lizards and birds. I studied the curly-tailed green lizard like a scientist. I especially loved the chameleon, however, and how it blended in through camouflage with its surroundings. I would watch how it changed color and waited for its prey, devouring insects with its perfectly projected tongue.

As for birds, they are very strategic builders. They identify perfect spots to build protective nests for their eggs and young ones and coordinate their beaks and claws to achieve their goals. I was intrigued by the coordination of the feeding process by the parents, ensuring that the young ones enjoyed their scrumptious meal of worms. Some birds nested on the ground where their eggs were protected by the special rock formations; so, too, are the Abaco Parrots. As an adult, on my visits to Great Inagua, I observed the parrots nesting in the trees. I am still fascinated by the parrots in Inagua, picking and holding almonds with one foot and feeding themselves while holding onto a tree limb with the firmly wrapped claws of the other. Unlike the Abaco Parrots, their natural habitat is the trees.

I took my time and walked slowly on these treks, allowing me to be at one with nature. School, which I liked and tended to always place in the top three every year, taught me the basics. But the environment and people really taught me the skills I had no idea I would need later to be an elite Crime Scene Investigator (CSI). For example, when I was a forensic crime scene investigator, it occurred to me that I had a natural knack because of all the times I kneeled down and observed those small animals and insects in their natural habitats.

Early Education

Formal school was interesting enough. I had a teacher, I remember in class two, who spanked me in the palm of my hand with a twelve-inch ruler. Our head teacher, Mr. Norman Archer, was assisted by monitors who were older students. I remember Mrs. Maggie Del Saunders-McDonald, Mrs. Pet Prichard-Gardiner, Mr. Hubert Ingraham, Miss Shirley, and Miss Genevieve Archer as some of my tutors and school monitors. Mr. Ingraham was later elected to Parliament as a Progressive Liberal Party member, and later he became the Rt. Honorable Prime Minister, leading a Free National Movement government. My brother, Everette, was my chief mentor and at-home tutor. I also fondly remember headmasters Mr. Norman Archer and later Mr. Bertram Stuart. Mr. Norman Archer was the victim of a rebellion by some of the parents. It was an unfortunate incident. I can still hear my mother crying over the strange happening. Mr. Stuart was sent to replace him. Stuart was later assisted by two Eleuthera natives, Mr. Donald Symonette and Mr. James Moultrie. Symonette went on to lead The Bahamas Union of Teachers at one point, and James Moultrie went on to become a parliamentarian and diplomat under the Progressive Liberal Party and later an Anglican priest.

The arrival of Stuart, Symonette, and Moultrie brought a new perspective to education in our community and an excitement to learn. It also saw the return of some of our bright students who had left at a very early age. Returning as school monitors were James Edgecombe, Alphonso Wright, Clyde Cornish, Ejnar Cornish, and a student from Cedar Harbour All Age School, Austin Mills. There was a rejuvenation of interest in learning. I can vividly remember the senior and some junior students gathering under the streetlight in Bootle Town nightly. Some were working through mathematical problems in the street. There were three notable young men: Ronald Murray, Brian McIntosh, and Maxwell Rolle; these students were sharp. I don't remember anyone else working out the problems as quickly as they did. I thought Maxwell Rolle was a genius. He was brilliant in all subjects. Mr. Symonette and Mr. Moultrie got us involved in all aspects of education and sports.

That one time when I got a spanking on my hand, I took my complaint to my brother, Everette. I believe this was one of my first lessons on authority. I thought Everette was going to "rough up" the teacher for me because he was much bigger than my teacher. But instead, Everette questioned me about the backstory of the hand spanking. It was clear that I deserved the reprimand because I was disruptive in class. So, Everette scolded me again and warned me to always be respectful and to pay attention in class. Once again, the experience helped shape me as an officer, as I always wanted to be on the right side of a situation, to be able to report the facts as they are, and to uphold rules.

The school day always ended just in time. The journey home was much quicker. I looked forward to a home-cooked meal and a swim in the beautiful turquoise ocean waters.

Chapter 5
PREPARATION FOR GLOBAL CHALLENGES

We were taught to swim from around the age of three by our cousin Elmore Sawyer, nicknamed "Forty." Forty was our hero. He was the best all-around young man in our town, probably in the world to us younger ones, if you asked. He was a skilled boat handler, a fast car driver, and made everything look easy. Growing up, he made it his responsibility to prepare the boys of the community for swimming, driving, and operating small boats. Forty hadn't spent many years in school. It is rumored that Forty's astuteness placed him in a higher category than the well-educated ones among us. He also demonstrated that there is more to education than formal schooling. Forty has shown that he is the most intelligent, skilled, and compassionate human being I know.

As we were growing up, Forty was gone a lot. He captained boats and luxury yachts in The Bahamas and the United States of America. He captained yachts across the Atlantic Ocean from Europe, by way of the Caribbean chain, into The Bahamas. He was renowned for his skills as one of the best captains to hail from Abaco. I recall a story where the captain of a new, huge 160-foot luxury yacht from the United States yielded to the assistance of Sawyer to enter the Treasure Cay Marina. Because of Elmore's reputation, the yacht's owner requested Forty's services. With such ease, Forty came to the rescue, entered the bridge of the vessel, and moored it like clockwork. I spoke to Forty about this incident. He informed me that he first met the captain, who at the time was a maritime student at a college in New Jersey, USA. The student would come by the marina often, and he would teach the college student about the different equipment and operations of the yacht. Unfortunately, the captain was killed in a traffic mishap in Florida in the prime of his life.

Just like nature, I see Forty as one of my greatest teachers. He not only helped to mold my character, but he taught me so much about life, how to balance between family, friends, and fun. He taught me how to ride a bicycle, and he even taught me how to drive a stick-shift truck at age nine. Yes! Elmore "Forty" Sawyer and Boynell "Chubby" Williams, my first cousins, are two sharers of many of my life's key lessons. Boynell taught me how to survive in the city, having relocated to Nassau at the age of seventeen. He was tall and quite handsome, the ladies' man, well-dressed. Loud with many stories to tell; the ladies were intrigued by this. He drew crowds to his presence when he spoke. He is gifted with an amazing memory, charming, and a fun guy to be around. He would always give me sound advice to keep me focused.

Chapter 6
POLITICS

At around age ten or eleven, my interest shifted to politics. The political storm of the Progressive Liberal Party and the labor movement was intensifying in The Bahamas at the time. Majority rule was on the horizon. The then-government, the United Bahamian Party, was very popular in Abaco, with three elected members of Parliament: Captain Leonard Thompson, Mr. Frank Christie, and Mr. John Bethel; they were all white Bahamians. I must say that this whole issue regarding race became more pronounced in Abaco because of partisan politics. Blacks in Abaco tended to be more neutral and independent in their thinking. We didn't immediately identify with racial equality and the need for jobs and social acceptance among the majority of blacks in Nassau. But eventually, black Abaconians began to get swept up in the majority rule movement.

I started hanging around the older gentlemen in the community who had access to radios and newspapers that reported political news. Mr. Clarence Poitier was a local store owner; we affectionately called him Uncle Poitier, and he was well-versed in politics in The Bahamas and internationally. He would take the time to explain certain issues to me. Of course, in the United States, the civil rights movement was topical. I can say that I was influenced by both movements. I couldn't wait to go and listen to the radio newscast with Uncle Poitier. And I always picked up the newspapers he was done with so that I could read more closely.

It would be my father's first cousin, Mr. Sherlin Bootle, encouraged and supported by some family, who would try his hand at politics first. He ran as an independent in the pivotal 1967 General Elections, which saw the formation of a coalition government by a former United Bahamian Party (UBP) member, Mr. Alvin Braynen, and Labor Party member, Mr. Randol Fawkes. Sherlin and many members of our family were not PLP supporters in that election. I campaigned with him throughout North Abaco as an independent. He would call my father "Jenkins," and I was called "Lil Jenkins." He faced the UBP giants, Leonard Thompson, Frank Christie, and John Bethel, losing marginally. But his performance was so impressive that it caught the attention of the new premier, Lynden Pindling. Following the death of Hon. Uriah McPhee, Member of Parliament for the Shirlea Constituency, the premier sought a new mandate from the Bahamian people in 1968.

My brother Everette and cousin Joseph Sawyer, both PLPs at the time, were directed to have Sherlin meet with the premier. Hon. Sherlin Bootle went on to be elected as a PLP in 1968 and 1972. He served as Deputy Speaker of the House of Assembly during part of his tenure. In 1977, another cousin replaced him as the PLP representative for the Cooper's Town constituency. The Hon. Hubert A. Ingraham was later expelled from the Progressive Liberal Party after he boldly spoke out against the scandal, corruption, and drug allegations emanating from the 1984 Commission of Inquiry that hit The Bahamas like an earthquake. He later became prime minister of the country in 1992, leading the Free National Movement to victory.

Family Political Bloodline

Warren J. Levarity, MP; Sherlin C. Bootle, MP; The Rt. Hon. Hubert Ingraham, PM, MP; Kirk Cornish, MP; Fritz Bootle, Candidate; Felix Sawyer, Candidate; and I, Candidate.

Reading the papers, listening to the radio, and campaigning with my cousin gave me a social consciousness and ignited a fire in my spirit. There were older men in the community like JBJC who swore by my reports. If I didn't say it, it wasn't so. They waited to hear from me about what was happening locally, nationally, and internationally. And I was so excited to oblige. I grew extremely passionate about politics and adamant about the promises made and delivered to our people. For this reason, I was active. One can only imagine the disappointment: election after election, promises every five years, and the basic infrastructure, like roads, water, and lights, were not fulfilled. My father, Prince III, was a campaign general for an independent candidate, Mr. Colin Reese, a local businessman from Bermuda.

Abaco Secession Attempt

It was interesting that little fringe groups started to pop up in Abaco. One such group that caught the attention of the country was headed by Mr. Errington "Bumpy" Watkins, Mr. Chuck Hall, and Mr. Bert Williams. This secessionist group's sole focus heading into the 1972 general elections was to stop the Pindling-led government from successfully including Abaco as a part of an independent Bahamas while they petitioned England for the country's independence from Great Britain.

Domestic Work Experience

Prior to the 1972 General Elections, I worked as a bar waiter and wine steward at the Treasure Cay Beach Hotel. I was a little too young when I started, but no one really checked; maybe it was because of my mature look. Mr. Leon Johnson, the chief bartender, taught me the skills of the profession: mix drinks, understand the different assortments of wines, and develop people skills when dealing with bar customers. My wine steward duties were during dinner time. Boy, he would oversee us like a hawk, ensuring we never mixed-up orders or spilled anything. He had a keen eye for detail and was a perfectionist.

I was eventually hired as the chief bartender by Mr. Kenneth Major Sr., a well-respected building contractor and the owner and operator of the Major's Hilltop Hotel in Cooper's Town. The establishment was a beautifully built structure in a prime location. Mr. Major had a vision for the community, and it appeared that he was onto something great. I am grateful for the confidence that Major Sr. placed in me, giving me my very first opportunity in management in 1971. Sadly, that local historic establishment was destroyed by fire in 2001.

Additionally, quite skilled with the keyboard, I was part of a musical group that was also hired by the Treasure Cay Beach Hotel. A few of us got together in high school and became known as the "Everyday People" band. Harrison Sands was the vocalist, and Millet Kemp was the drummer. Both were my cousins and best friends. The band was quite popular. There were several other talented musicians—cousins and friends: Rudy Cornish, James Lightbourne, Maxwell Rolle, Harold Grant. We were recorded and featured on ZNS Radio with Mr. Charles Carter on his Young Bahamian show. We also recorded a forty-five vinyl record with singer William Bill Humes featuring the "Goombay Beat" and the "Goombay Shimmey." Harrison Sands recorded a local hit, "Paying the Bills." It got playing time on ZNS.

Night of the Explosions

All of these factors I mention shaped the young adolescent I became who was standing on the dock at Marsh Harbour on the night when a never concretely identified crew decided to carry through plans to set off explosives and possibly kill the young premier and many others in their bid for total secession from a country laboring to become independent. And on that fateful night, I made a decision, as life had guided me to that point, to leave Abaco and move into New Providence to apply to the Royal Bahamas Police Force to become an officer.

I knew then that I wanted to be on the right side of law and order in my country. I knew that I wanted to be a patriotic member of a nation that was self-determined and progressive. For me, the decision was clear. At the time, we had no military. If we did, it was likely I would have applied the next day to serve my country. But we had a police force. And even though this meant that I would have to leave my parents and the comfort and ease of Abaco, particularly Cooper's Town, built by my grandfather, it was unavoidable for me. I was going to become a policeman.

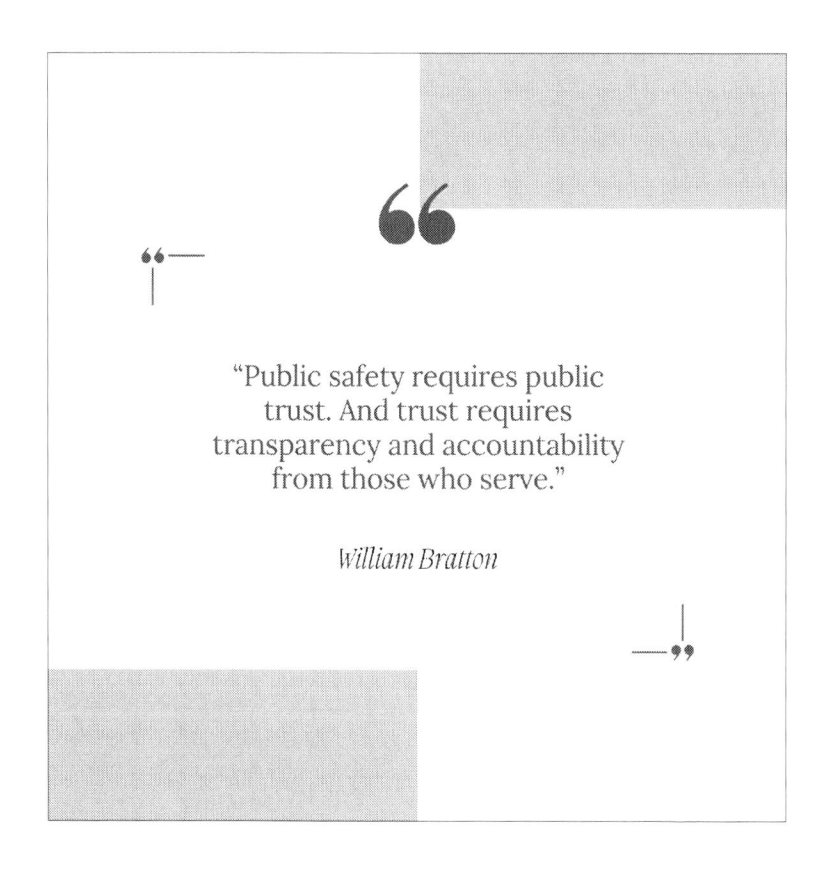

"Public safety requires public trust. And trust requires transparency and accountability from those who serve."

William Bratton

Chapter 7
THE ROAD TO INDEPENDENCE

The United Bahamian Party (UBP) achieved self-governance through a series of constitutional and political steps, attaining internal self-government on January 7, 1964. The political happenings in Abaco really intensified during the 1972 election campaign. The Progressive Liberal Party (PLP) had secured itself in the 1968 elections. The margin of victory was just too slim the year prior as a coalition government. Gerrymandering was a contentious issue criticized by the Progressive Liberal Party in opposition. However, this issue continued as the new government prepared for elections and the boundaries authority made changes. The year 1962 had given universal suffrage, allowing adult Bahamians of both genders to vote. This was spearheaded by women of all political persuasions: PLP, UBP, Labour, and Independent. I know in Abaco there were women who were fighting for the right to vote. Beforehand, only men who owned property were eligible. There is a thought that local gerrymandering through the boundaries authority made it almost impossible for fair elections.

When the premier called the April 10, 1968, elections, it was to give him breathing room and a stronger grip on the reins of power. The results were more conclusive: 85.5% of the electorate turned out to vote and the Progressive Liberal Party won 29 of the 38 constituencies.

But shortly after, internal rumblings in the Progressive Liberal Party led to a heated split. Eight members (the Dissident 8) of high rank who questioned the ruling tactics of the young premier left the PLP in 1970. The Free PLP joined forces with the remaining disbanded United Bahamian Party and some members of the National Democratic Party to form the Free National Movement (FNM) in 1971, with Sir Cecil Wallace Whitfield as the founding member and the first leader of the FNM.

The 1972 General Election was not just a referendum on independence; it was a heated rivalry between former comrades who, less than five years prior, pooled their energies for the noble attainment of black majority rule. The splintering of the Progressive Liberal Party was also mired in violence. There had been a fight down in Lewis Yard, Grand Bahama, in November 1970, where ardent Pindling supporters struck two FNM members with chairs. Sir Cecil Wallace Whitfield, then serving in Pindling's Cabinet, along with the local representative Maurice Moore, were attacked as a strong message from PLP supporters over rumors that they were trying to undermine the Pindling-led government. This sealed the fallout.

After the formation of the Free National Movement, competing interests intensified the opposition. Arguably, independence became a political football. The 1972 elections, often described as a referendum on independence, were also a test for the newly formed party, the Free National Movement. Undoubtedly, the UBP had set the stage for independence.

The argument for this is strengthened by the fact that constitutional advances had already brought The Bahamas to the precipice of internal self-government in 1964. The colony convened its first Parliament way back in 1729. Political stability and the gradual development of governance over time, aside from the complete inclusion of black individuals, resulted in a conference in 1963. This occurred shortly after the UBP retained governance in 1962, despite universal suffrage being in place. At this convening, it was agreed that, except for foreign affairs, defense, and internal security, the colony should have full internal self-government.

On the ground in Abaco between 1971 and 1972, the political division became pronounced. My family and I, given Sherlin's alliance, were very much supportive of him. The UBP was no more, but its agents and supporters remained powerful, and their political philosophies now seemed justifiable because no one could point to race or economics anymore. Black men originally from the PLP were now radically opposed to the PLP and began the "corruption" labeling. Still, the narrative swiftly shifted to whether it was too soon for independence. The FNM slogan became, "Independence—But Not Now!"

I was a recent high school graduate at the time, just settling into bartending and the artistry of music. But everywhere I went, every discussion I had—at the restaurants, on the dock, even at the dinner table—Bahamians of all walks of life were debating the pros and cons of independence. Some were pushing the fear advanced by people like Sir Stafford Sands, former UBP Cabinet Minister, father of tourism and financial services, who left The Bahamas not long after their 1967 defeat. He openly expressed before he left that he had no confidence in the PLP running the country. Many Bahamians, especially after the very public fallout happening in the governing PLP, started to wonder if maybe he was right.

But then there were proud ordinary Bahamians who had marched in the struggle and believed, like young Premier Pindling, Carlton Francis, Arthur Hanna, Cecil Wallace Whitfield, and the other freedom fighters, that independence was as natural as the next step in walking. They understood the law, constitutional advances, and nation-building. The father of Bahamianization, the Hon. A. D. Hanna, although married to an Englishwoman, could not imagine the true self-determination of the ordinary Bahamian without the attainment of independence. The other more progressive countries in the Caribbean had already successfully attained independence. He was one of the framers of what the relationship between Britain and an independent Bahamas would look like. He understood that, in its simplicity, retaining allegiance with Great Britain would be a formality only—as the new equivalent to the British governor, who was vested with enormous but waning power at the time, would be symbolic power now vested in a Bahamian son or daughter essentially acting in accordance with the Bahamian Parliament.

Explosions

Among unlearned Bahamians, the argument was sensationalized, and campaigning for the 1972 elections turned into a mudslinging fiasco, questioning the very essence of dignity and humanity among colored men. That is how what happened in Abaco leading up to the 1972 general elections came to be. Some powerful men of Abaco allegedly convinced a handful of anti-PLP radicals to set explosives around the area where Pindling and the PLP would be holding a rally. And as fate would have it, I was nearby.

There was much talk of Abaconians wanting to secede from the rest of the country. There were even suspicions that foreign interests were involved. Rumors spread that these interests were willing to go to extremes to hurt, even kill. I had heard about it but didn't believe it. Harrison Sands, Millet Kemp, and I decided to attend the PLP meeting held on the grounds of the Government Dock at Marsh Harbor, Abaco, on this fateful night. There were three explosions: one in the graveyard near the local police station and two in the harbor near the meeting site. Luckily, the fourth one, which was loaded in a tin tub, didn't go off. That one came up against a steel-hulled boat moored at the dock, and by the grace of God, did not ignite. If it had, it would've been catastrophic. There would've been much damage and possibly even loss of lives.

As from that day to this, no group or individual has ever gone to that degree of violence in our country to make a public political statement. Many cars leaving that meeting experienced malicious tire damage. An airplane owned by a PLP supporter received gunshot damage at the Marsh Harbour International Airport. Several heavy-duty roadwork pieces of equipment also received gunshot damage. The night was wild; police and civilians were running for dear life. The premier was safely guarded and swiftly removed from that location.

Training

My training started at Police Headquarters, East Street, Nassau, along with twenty-nine (29) other young Bahamians in their late teens or early twenties. The officers hailed from Abaco in the north to Inagua in the south. The administration at the Training School was headed by Mr. McDonald Fields, Superintendent of Police, a Trinidadian, a massive gentleman who appeared to be about 6' 7", with a military look, and Mr. Garnett Beneby, Assistant Superintendent of Police, a smaller gentleman. They were the ones who interviewed me for the position. They were both firm in their questioning and the charge they gave me. It gave me a fairly good idea of what to expect. I was a successful candidate.

The training staff was made up of Chief Inspector Mr. Vernon Wilkinson, Chief Drill Instructor, and Inspector Mr. Kemuel Hepburn, Chief Classroom Instructor. Drill Instructors included Staff Sergeant 391 Henry Thurston, Sergeant 352 Acel Clark, Corporal 134 E. Dean, and 513 Arlie Forbes. Class Instructors were Sergeant 341 Ervin Taylor, Woman Sergeant 363 Dorothy Davis, Sergeant 133 Leon Johnson, Sergeant 275 Alfred Williams, and our squad instructor, Sergeant 23 Edmund Stubbs. The force education officer was Mr. Vincent Wilson, assisted by Corporal 74 Colby. Corporal Vincent Charlton was the Clerk. The Force Medical Officer was Staff Sergeant Nelson Stubbs.

At the time, we had no idea that we would be a part of the greatest historical event in The Bahamas. We started our training at the amazing historic Police Headquarters on East Street, where the Training School was located at that time. We were introduced to the noble history of the organization. At this time, the Royal Bahamas Police Force was celebrating 132 years as a law enforcement agency. At this historic site, some of us were assigned to live in Arthur's House. The building once served as a prison. The accoutrements of the gallows were still in place.

The whole compound was fascinating to the inquiring mind. So much so that each building had its unique story. The dining and canteen areas were photographic museums; they told the true stories of where we came from as an organization. Photographs that stood out to me were the ones showing the removal of the Cuban flag from Cay Sal, which was replaced by the Union Jack. The Cuban authorities claimed that Cay Sal was part of their territory. The local officers could be seen holding their rifles, standing beside the Union Jack in a defensive position. The country was then the responsibility of Great Britain. I knew that in an independent nation, the responsibility for protection rested with the Royal Bahamas Police Force. There was no military force at the time. I was prepared to hold that defensive position in the future, carrying the Bahamian flag.

This became clear to me in May 1980 when the HMBS Flamingo was destroyed by Cuban military MiG fighter jets off Ragged Island while heading toward Cay Santo Domingo with Cuban poachers in tow on their boat. We lost four of our military heroes in that incident: Fenrick Sturrup, Austin Smith, David Tucker, and Edward Williams. I was alone on duty at the Criminal Records Office on Sunday, May 11, 1980, the day after the incident. The Police Control Center contacted the office to have personnel on standby to travel to that site. It was later decided that it would be too risky for us to travel into that area.

We completed three months of training at Police HQ, East Street, before moving on to the new training location in Oakes Field. This was a major upgrade from where we came from. We were the last squad to train and graduate under British rule, and the first to train and graduate from the New Police Training

College in Oakes Field, an independence gift from the British Government.

After three additional months of training at the Oakes Field campus, the squad graduated. In a closely contested race for the prestigious Baton of Honour, Constable 925 Tyrone Morris won it by ¼ point over me. We were fortunate to be tutored by some of the brightest minds in the organization at the time. One of our instructors, Sergeant 275 Alfred Williams, was known as the "Walking Penal Code." Of course, we challenged him as others did. However, his brilliance was remarkable.

Our training was intense, to say the least. The drill instructors were on a mission for perfection in preparing us for the upcoming independence celebrations. Upon graduating from the Police Training College in April 1973, our unit "C" Squad 72/73 received high praise for our drill skills, which were described as phenomenal. We were assigned to the Internal Security Division, Oakes Field, to complete our rigorous training with Deputy Superintendent Mr. Keith Mason and his team. We were mandated to carry out the Rifle Party drill duties in full ceremonial dress. "C" Squad passed the test and earned the right to lead this national event. We are forever grateful to the cadre of dynamic drill instructors; their hard work and dedication were second to none.

First Honor Guard

We were now ready to meet a prince. Our first assignment was to form the honor guard for HRH Prince Charles, the Prince of Wales. We assembled on Prince George Wharf in the open space near the old Customs shed and the Churchill Building on July 6, 1973. The squad marched to the location of the dais to await HRH's arrival, where the prince would take his royal salute. The Prince of Wales arrived shortly thereafter, having disembarked from the HMS Minerva, berthed at Prince George Dock. He conducted the inspection of our unit before proceeding to Rawson Square and Government House.

Honor guard for HRH Prince Charles, the Prince of Wales. Welbourne Bootle, 3rd officer in the front rank from the right marker.

Chapter 8
JULY 10, 1973

While we were busy training to become the country's newest crop of police officers, the Pindling-led PLP Government, handsomely reelected in 1972, was busily confirming the symbols of a new nation. Several competitions were held to invite Bahamian talent to play a role in the composition of the national anthem and pledge that would represent a new country. A few years before independence, the colony was already renamed as the Commonwealth of the Bahama Islands. However, with independence, the country's name became The Commonwealth of Bahamas.

The national fish was identified as the blue marlin; the national bird was the flamingo, and the national flower and tree became the yellow elder and the lignum vitae. The government of the country also decided on a coat of arms, made of many things indigenous to the country. The motto on the coat of arms is a reminder of the direction in which it is hoped the country would always go: "forward, upward, onward, together."

Our national anthem was written by the late educator, Timothy Gibson, and is thus:

Lift up your head to the rising sun, Bahamaland;
March on to glory, your bright banners waving high.
See how the world marks the manner of your bearing.
Pledge to excel through love and unity.

Pressing onward, march together to a common loftier goal;
Steady sunward, tho the weather hide the wide and treacherous shoal.

Lift up your head to the rising sun, Bahamaland;
'Til the road you've trod lead unto your God,
March on, Bahamaland.

It was also decided to have a less popular national song, "God Bless Our Sunny Clime," composed by Timothy Gibson and Clement Bethel and written by Rev. Philip Rahming:

God bless our sunny clime, spur us to height sublime.
To keep men free, let brothers, sisters stand
Firm, trusting hand in hand, throughout Bahamaland
One brotherhood, one brotherhood.
Let gratefulness ascend, courageous deed extend
From isle to isle. Long let us treasure peace,
So may our lives increase, our prayers never cease.
Let freedom ring! Let freedom ring!
The long, long night has passed, the morning breaks at last,
From shore to shore, sunrise with golden gleam
Sons n' daughters share the dream, for one working team
One brotherhood, one brotherhood.
Not for this time nor for this chosen few alone
We pledge ourselves. Live loyal to our God.
Love country, friend and foe, oh help us by thy might!
Great God our King! Great God our King!

The Pledge of Allegiance was written by Rev. Philip Rahming and is as follows:

I pledge my allegiance to the flag and to the Commonwealth of The Bahamas for which it stands, one people united in love and service.

The bahamaslibraries.org describes our national flag as:

> The design of the Bahamian Flag is a black equilateral triangle against the mast superimposed on a horizontal background made up of two colors on three equal stripes, aquamarine, gold, and aquamarine.
>
> Black, as strong color, represents the vigor and force of a united people; the triangle pointing represents the enterprise and determination of the Bahamian people to develop and process the rich resources of land and sea, symbolized by gold and aquamarine respectively.

I can remember July 9, 1973, just like it was yesterday. Although it was the start of my career, I must say that it was my ultimate highlight. What an honor it was to be among that number of people at our very first independence celebration on Clifford Park. Bahamians continue to look forward to the annual celebration, much of which remains the same in terms of programming.

Thousands gather at Clifford Park each year for an ecumenical service of thanksgiving, the Governor General's inspection of the honor guard, and the hoisting of the Bahamian flag at midnight on July 10. While there have been some additions to the ceremony over the years, such as the castle, performances by the police auto and K-9 units, as well as skits, poetry, and choir performances, the gist and feeling remain the same each year. The attendance of so many ordinary Bahamians encourages me that we are still a deeply patriotic people. I just pray that we can inspire Bahamians to put this patriotism into action, love, and community advancement. Additionally, it has always been my hope that we can expand the Bahamian experience and historical accomplishments to capture the significance of all the many Bahamian islands. Thankfully, they all now have an independence service, but the observances, like that first independence season, are still so New Providence-centric.

Getting back to that first July 10 ceremony, it began for my squad weeks before with rigorous training. There might have been some exhaustion on July 9, but the adrenaline was even stronger. I woke up that morning focused on my uniform. The tunic was white and had to be ironed perfectly—not just because it would come under inspection from my superiors, but later from the new governor general, Bahamian-born Sir Milo B. Butler. The perfection of my uniform was, for me, a reflection of my pride and honor. Just as I had presented myself to HRH Prince Charles, I felt even more pressured to be immaculate for my new country.

My uniform and tunic were well starched. My belt, helmet, and boots were so polished that they shone like glass. The brass buttons, steel bayonet, spike, and chain sparkled like stars. I practiced in and out of the mirror in my room for hours, ensuring I would not be prone to any mistakes. My poor legs were overworked, although in fine condition. They would shake a little later, but only out of nerves.

Around 10 p.m. on July 9, we reported to the Internal Security Division of the RBPF to be transported to Clifford Park by bus. You have to imagine what it was like for our group, many still teenagers and the others in their very early twenties. We were hardly men—still trading stories of what it was like to welcome HRH Prince Charles. Ego is sometimes a gift, as that was perhaps the only factor preventing any of us from crying tears of immense patriotism and passing out from the fear of how our duties might be carried out and received.

In this moment, it was hard not to somehow feel chosen by something beyond the RBPF. We felt as though fate and our faith in God had chosen us from before our births for this fateful night, as our country transitioned from being ruled by someone else to being self-ruled. I couldn't help but think of my personal journey as the grandson of Prince Albert Bootle Jr. and Eliza Baillou Bootle. I thought about Sidney's young death and the impact this still had on my life, my peculiar personality, and life growing up in Abaco. I had been traveling to Nassau throughout my young life, especially as a travel companion to my mother whenever she went. But here I was in my own independence, settling into manhood as the first squad to be affirmed in what was in a few moments to become, the Commonwealth of The Bahamas.

As the many young Bahamians on the bus with me had to be thinking about how their lineage had come to The Bahamas as slaves and how, over a century and a half, battles for equality had been waged, I too thought of the journey of my fore-parents, my great-great-grandfather Pa Mussa from West Africa to America to West Grand Bahama, Pa Prince Albert I and Sarah Russell Bootle, and then Prince Albert Bootle Jr. and Eliza Baillou Bootle to Abaco. Our history varied in how much freedom and equality our families had each endured, as there were officers who had hailed from other Out Islands. However, our present was the same. We would be issued passports now, which would mark our nationality as fully Bahamian.

And what of all the pre-independence debates for and against independence, and the explosions—what did it all mean now? I believe, secretly, that there was a feeling of great pride even in the bellies of those who claimed that we needed to wait. Some of them were gathered in the park as well. But we, on the bus, set apart to join the flag and the dignitaries, to be a significant part of the ceremony, would forever be special. No one could ever take this historic achievement away from us. We would go down in history as the first! We marched on as subjects and marched off as Bahamians.

The time had arrived. The parade was given the order to fall in and line up at the western end of the park for a pre-inspection and roll call prior to the "March on!" This was a proud moment. Butterflies took over my belly and we were all beaming with patriotism as the command was given, "Forward march!" With chests out and rifles on our shoulders, our platoon led the parade on to Clifford Park behind the Royal Bahamas Police Force Band. Deputy Superintendent of Police, Mr. Keith Mason, was the parade commander. Superintendent Dennis Morgan was the director of the Police Band. We marched on to the thunderous applause from the crowd at around 11:00 p.m. HRH Prince Charles arrived at the park at precisely 11:15 p.m.

Now, there are many stories of potential mishaps on that night which are questionable, to say the least. One is that the official flag was accidentally left behind. Not so. The flag bearer, Sergeant Ervin Taylor, was in possession of the official Bahamian flag fifteen minutes before the ceremony. Another claim is that Sir Milo Butler had left it at Government House in his bedroom. The British Governor, Sir John Paul, had not yet been replaced by Sir Milo Butler. Sir Milo was therefore not the occupant of Government House.

My position in the unit was third from the right marker, in the front rank. The parade was given the command, "Parade halt!" In unison, we came to a thunderous stop. The crowd screamed out in applause. The crowd of over 60,000 went wild when the right marker, Staff Sergeant 391 Henry Thurston, made a sharp right turn and lifted his left knee parallel to his left shoulder. For the first time in my life, I heard the stentorian sound of a crowd.

The midnight hour was fast approaching and then the time was upon us. The parade was given the command, "Attention!" by Deputy Superintendent of Police, Keith Mason. Standing a few feet away from the flag, we were commanded to give a Royal Salute to the British flag as it was lowered to the sound of God Save the Queen. Then, the time arrived! The Bahamian flag was now boldly taking its official, rightful position on the prestigious tall, lanky pole. What happened next to me was unexpected. The national anthem of The Bahamas played officially for the first time— "March on Bahama Land." The feeling was one of exuberance, flowing with emotions; it was the most thrilling feeling I had ever experienced. My heart was pulsating and the palms of my hands holding the rifle were wet with sweat, as tears and sweat flowed down my face. It was like an electrical shock deep in my belly. This feeling was indescribable—an explosion of overwhelming joy. There were goosebumps as I shivered, witnessing the hoisting of the Bahamian flag up close and personal; beaming with pride, I realized that this moment in time would never be repeated!

The Union Jack was lowered by Sergeant 275 Alfred Williams and the Bahamian flag was hoisted by Sergeant 341 Ervin Taylor, our law lecturers at the Police College, both brilliant men. The timing of lowering one and raising the other was synchronized perfectly. The Bahamian flag reached the top of the pole at exactly midnight as the new national anthem began to play. The night was still and calm, humid with no wind! However, almost immediately, the flag began to wave with a breeze that came as though the angels were saying, "Well done, Bahamas!" The rumor of a fan or contraption to make the flag wave is a myth. I had an upfront view of the area and flagpole. I confirmed this with retired Deputy Commissioner of Police, Mr. Keith Mason.

My experience was priceless! Giving the First General Salute to our national flag and simultaneously hearing the new national anthem being played while in the General Salute position, with a rifle and bayonet held in front of me, was the highlight of my career!

We performed a farewell honor guard for Sir John Paul, the last British royal governor and the first governor general of The Bahamas, at the Nassau International Airport. It was an honor and with great pride that my squad formed the guard of honor for the first Bahamian governor general, Sir Milo Butler, in August 1973. This ceremony took place in Rawson Square. Our squad was called upon frequently to perform many ceremonies afterward, including visits from Queen Elizabeth II of Great Britain, President Yakubu Gowon of Nigeria, and other foreign state visits, Supreme Court openings, changing of the guard every fortnight, and other assigned duties.

We were delighted to be the first to give the father of our new nation, our new prime minister, Sir Lynden Oscar Pindling, a general salute, with the sound of our national anthem being played in the background.

The unit was comprised of some of the Force's most dedicated officers:

PC 923 John Rolle, PC 924 Patrick Levarity, PC 925 Tyrone Morris, PC 926 Jacob Hanna, PC 927 Samuel Rodgers, PC 928 James Taylor, PC 929 Samuel Johnson, PC 930 David Thompson, PC 933 Edward Wilson, PC 934 David Knowles, PC 935 Burntle Max Charlton, PC 936 Carlton Butler, PC 937 Lionel Forbes, PC 938 Audi Murphy, PC 939 Rodney McKenzie, PC 941 Noel McPhee, PC 942 Patrick Brown, PC 943 Thaddeus Rolle, PC 944 Welbourne C. Bootle, PC 945 Brunell Cartwright, PC 946 Nolan Dean, PC 947 James Major, PC 948 Harrison Sands, PC 949 David Johnson, PC 950 Wellington Wright, PC 951 Phillip Carrol, and PC 953 Carrington McIntosh.

Three did not graduate: PC 931 Montgomery Kemp-Brown, PC 932 Joe Johnson, and PC 940 Nelson Scott.

Post-Independence

Fifty-plus years later, are we really an independent nation? Or are we too dependent on outsiders for survival? Did we do enough to uplift our people from where they were pre-independence to where they should be? What sustainable programs did we implement in the inner city? How successful are they? The rise of the phoenix is still an illusion. Are we giving incentives for Over-the-Hill business personnel without all the red tape to establish themselves? And to encourage employment and training for the future entrepreneurs?

I walked through the inner city via the track roads on police operations. This is where you see the real heart of the city. These are neglected areas that truly need sustainable attention—not handouts! I usually feel depressed when I traverse these areas. Fifty-plus years later, no Bahamian should be left behind. That's the message I understood Hanna, Pindling, and Whitfield (HPW) were conveying. No matter their different personalities or political views, they were singing from the same hymn sheet. My expectations are still high and alive. My

Bahamas must rise from the ashes and take that bold step with the passion that HPW had.

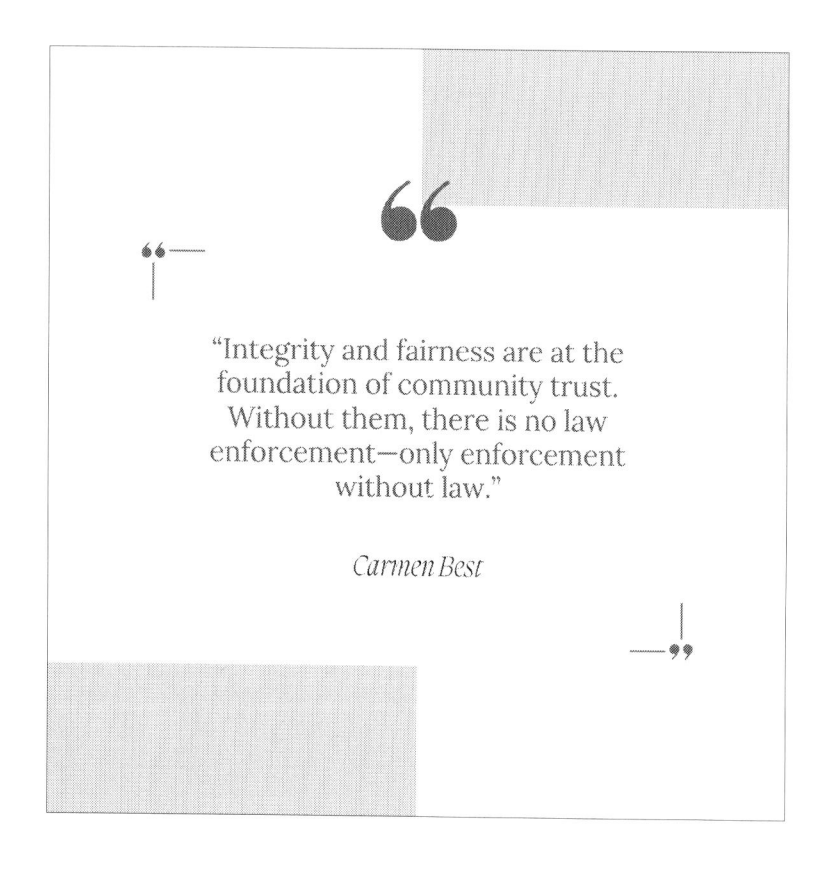

"Integrity and fairness are at the foundation of community trust. Without them, there is no law enforcement—only enforcement without law."

Carmen Best

Chapter 9
TRAINING

My service to this country was non-negotiable. Forty (40) years of dedicated professional service provided me with an invaluable education that no university could've taught. I called out sick less than ten days in forty years. I clocked close to three and a half years of unpaid overtime duties. I was assigned one orderly room charge because the police bus chauffeur collected our morning shift five minutes late from three outposts. No fault of the workers. However, we were all fined $5.00 each.

The Royal Bahamas Police Force was a beacon of discipline in The Bahamas. At the time I engaged as a recruit, it stood out as the longest serving law enforcement agency in the country. It carried out the duties of other agencies where they did not have a presence. The Marine Section carried out the duties of the Royal Bahamas Defence Force before its establishment. Many Officers from the Police Force Marine Section became a part of the Royal Bahamas Defence Force. The first Commodore, Mr. Leon Smith came from the Police Force Marine Section.

We were well represented by the British in 1972/73. Mr. John Hindmarsh served as Commissioner of Police. Mr. Stanley Moir was Sr. Assistant Commissioner. Mr. Dennis Morgan was Superintendent and Director of the Police Band. There were several other British officers serving at the time, heading various departments.

The training was an intense period during which discipline was instilled in the new officers. Recruits received physical training, self-defense, firearms education, law, constitution, court procedures, judging rules, social studies, and other pertinent developmental training. At that time, the recruits carried out their own domestic chores in the compound, classrooms, and dormitories. My understanding is that there was a change to that policy several years ago.

Crime Scene Training

During my early years of service, there was a major emphasis placed on training and retraining by the Force. Deserving officers with great potential and aptitude were sent for overseas training at the Federal Bureau of Investigation (FBI) Academy in Washington, DC, USA; Royal Canadian Mounted Police College (RCMP), Canada; and Bromsil, London, England, as well as several other five-star international police academies. Investigators and uniformed officers looked forward to the international training. Senior Assistant Commissioner of Police, Mr. Alonzo Butler, was far ahead of his time and recognized the

Detective Training Course the United Kingdom (L-R Detectives Lyndy Knowles, Welbourne Bootle, Perry Newton)

vision for a modern-day institution, twenty-first century policing. He was instrumental in having officers trained internationally. He made his mark as one of the brightest minds in the organization. He wanted to leave behind an educated agency; his efforts paid dividends.

I was a recipient who benefitted from his vision: training in Forensic Fingerprint Technology at the Royal Canadian Mounted Police College in Ottawa, Canada. I also trained in Forensic Crime Scene Investigation at the Metropolitan Detective Training School, Hendon, England. There, the photograph of Bahamian police officer, Mr. Bernard K. Nottage

Sr., was displayed on the alumni wall. This was a very proud moment for us, the Bahamian attendees. Additionally, I had training in Forensic Laser Fingerprint Technology at Texas Tech University, Lubbock, Texas, USA; Motorola Bio-Metric and Fingerprint Technology Training at Costa Mesa, California; and Printrak Automated Fingerprint Identification Technology, Anaheim, California. There were several additional training sessions by the International Association of Chiefs of Police and the International Association of Identification held at the Miami Beach Convention Centre and at Dorel, Miami, Florida.

On my Canadian and British training courses, Officer Lyndy Knowles of Mangrove Bush, Long Island, retired Superintendent of Police, accompanied me. We created a bond as working colleagues and very good friends over the years that still stands to this day. We speak on the telephone almost daily about different topical issues.

Posting

My first major posting was at the Southern Division on Market and Laird Street, where I faced practical policing. I went on foot patrol with senior constables who introduced me to the area. I remember vividly Constable Bert Perry, a huge man, who was The Bahamas' Heavyweight Boxing Champion at one time. I also worked with Mr. Nathaniel "Nat" Knowles, an outstanding amateur boxer and silver medalist at the Central American and Caribbean (CAC) Games. I had a feeling of comfort as I walked down Market Street to the Capitol Movie Theatre and the streets in between to Baillou Hill Road and East Street, Bain Town, Wulff Road, and the general areas. We had no firearms in those days, only a baton. This was a daily routine with different officers. Some days I was detailed to work at the Fox Hill, Cable Beach, the airport, or the Lyford Cay police stations. The officers took great pride in their work. The supervisors were on top of things, and complaints were dealt with expeditiously. The officers were well-versed in their subject matters and carried out their duties with excellence. At that time, training was paramount by the desk officers at the stations. Qualified officers were given the more serious tasks to carry out. There was always continuous training in process to prepare the weaker officers. Of course, there were slack ones among us; they were easily identifiable.

Soon, I was assigned as an inquiry officer, investigating complaints made at the newly constructed Coconut Grove Police Station. My mode of transportation was a Lambretta scooter. Investigations took me through Yellow Elder Gardens, Stapleton Gardens, Ridgeland Park, the Coconut Grove area, Montel Heights, and the general area of the station. Community policing was a natural function for the department.

I saw a decline in policing over the years, where quantity trumped quality. I witnessed, at times, where persons were recruited without having the requisite vetting done or basic qualifications. However, they were accepted and employed. I give credit to my other colleagues on the interview panel—respectable officers who noted all the flaws. However, against our advice at the time, unqualified persons were still hired. Many were hired who should never be in law enforcement. This contributed directly to the deterioration of the noble organization that boasted of loyalty, integrity, and courage. The decline was quite noticeable in performance and action.

The community suffers and national security is compromised when the powers that be bend the rules to fit a personal agenda! Some of the things officers get away with today are absolutely no surprise. We now see the result of what was planted: being senior in rank does not change who you are.

There was a time when you could identify an officer just by his or her respectful demeanor. Nowadays, this is not the case. Many officers are disrespectful to seniors in rank and the general public, disorderly, and showing no respect for law and order, with no fear of being seriously reprimanded for their actions. Sadly, in many cases, it appears to be the order of the day.

National Sovereignty Compromised

A Compstat meeting is held on a particular day of each week for comparing crime statistics, sharing information, responsibility, and accountability. The key is to improve effectiveness in crime-fighting methods. All major islands were online. This is an excellent tool for modern-day policing, once it is used for that intent. I was at the Freeport location when I advised the chairman at the Nassau location of some concerns I had with a large number of prisoners sent to The Bahamas without the normal vetting process. I thought this was a breach of our country's laws and a national security interest. How did the authorities accept anyone into The Bahamas without proof of citizenship? This would have been an easily verifiable process through fingerprints, any local address, birth, hospital and school records, and several other vetting procedures.

We had no antecedents or fingerprints on these allegedly very dangerous criminals. Surprisingly, a very high-ranking officer did not see the necessity for the vetting and saw nothing wrong with The Bahamas receiving them. The serious crime rate went up on Grand Bahama shortly thereafter, where high-powered rifles were used. These deportees allegedly had the paper Bahamian driver's licenses in their possession and were accepted as Bahamian citizens. The big question was, how were they issued and by whom? Sometime later, one of the deportees was arrested in Freeport for firearms possession along with his mother and sister. Even though officials accepted him as a born Bahamian, in his mother's statement, she said it was her first time visiting The Bahamas.

Observation

It is always disheartening when partisan politics becomes an influencing factor in a law enforcement organization; when the directives come from personal and politically motivated perspectives. You see it from both political parties, which destroys the very fiber of law enforcement. Over the years you expected this to happen. The sad part about this is that there are members of the Force who are pressured to support this, depending on the party in power. This demonstrates a lack of maturity, and the absence of values placed on our development as a country. Mediocrity is elevated, and excellent work ethic is overlooked.

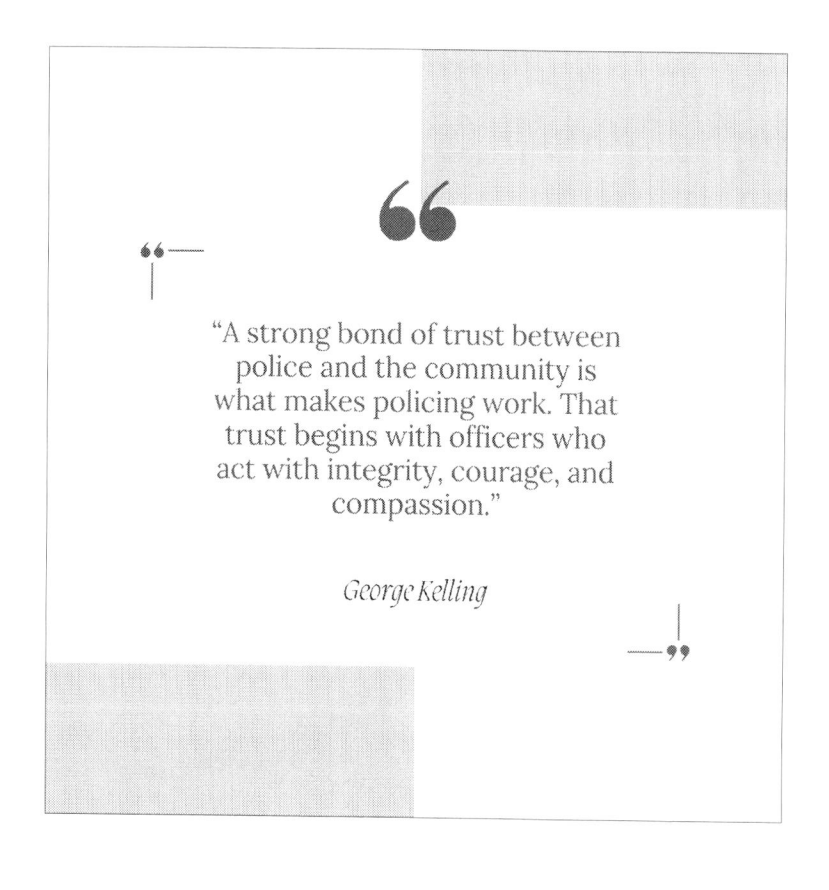

> "A strong bond of trust between police and the community is what makes policing work. That trust begins with officers who act with integrity, courage, and compassion."
>
> *George Kelling*

Chapter 10
SPECIAL UNIT MISSIONS

From 1977 to 1980, I was attached to the Internal Security Division as a member of a special unit that later became the Strike Force, Operation Bahamas Turks and Caicos (OBAT), in partnership with the United States Drug Enforcement Agencies. This was a very dark period in The Bahamas. Drug trafficking was at an all-time high. Our mission was to apprehend drug traffickers by patrolling the air and sea. We went on several high-profile missions from Great Inagua in the south to Walkers Cay, Abaco in the north.

Sometime in the late '70s, I was part of a major police and Defence Force raid on Norman's Cay in the Exumas. This mission became the topic of the now-famous 1984 Commission of Enquiry. On the original date, we gathered at the Internal Security Division of the Royal Bahamas Police Force to prepare for our travel to our targeted location. After several hours, we were advised that the operation was called off. Several days later, we were called back to the Internal Security Division without knowing where we were going. I was assigned to travel on one of the Defence Force vessels. Other officers were going in by aircraft. We left New Providence sometime after midnight and were briefed on where we were going around 3:15 a.m. Shortly afterward, we disembarked the ship and took up our positions on Norman's Cay, fully armed to face the danger ahead. I was disappointed when a Bahamian worker on the cay asked our team why we came so late. He advised that there were a lot of unusual movements by aircraft landing and taking off. He pointed out the warehouses that had been emptied.

Ironically, all of this took place on the day we were supposed to be on Norman's Cay. The cay was a haven for the notorious drug lord, Carlos Joe Lehder, and members of the Medellín Cartel headed by Pablo Escobar of Colombia. They had a 3,300-foot runway, with radars, attack dogs, and armed bodyguards. To think that someone in authority would put our lives in danger is unfathomable. The evidence at the 1984 Commission of Inquiry shed light on what took place and the level of corruption at the top levels of law enforcement and government. This, sadly, trickled down to the junior ranks. The hearing of the 1984 Commission of Inquiry brought light to the level of corruption that had infiltrated the very fabric of our society.

I ran into an officer at the Nassau International Airport on my way to an assignment. He was very disturbed as he told me about his transfer to a family island. To my shock and surprise, he mentioned a particular senior officer who called and advised him that he was responsible for his going to that island to act as an agent for him. He was to act as an agent for the senior officer, collecting gifts from questionable sources. The junior officer was a decent young man being corrupted by his superior. Obviously afraid, he needed someone to talk to whom he could trust. I advised him not to go against his principles and to focus on what he believes in.

It is sad when your trust level is limited to a few. I made the mistake of reporting a matter to the wrong person, whom I mistakenly believed was upright. I thought the matter was a major security threat to the sovereignty of The Bahamas. I could never have imagined how deep this ring went and the money and people involved. Sadly, some persons in authority were dishonest and could not care less about the consequences of their actions. Many years later in Freeport, a former police officer came and asked me to forgive him. I wanted to know why. He confessed that there was a hit out on me; and I should have been dead. He said that the execution had been given the green light. I wanted to know, why? He said I interrupted a huge operation; many people were upset about this. I became more convinced that I was covered by the grace of God through the prayers of my grandmother and mother.

My team went on several missions that were classified as highly dangerous. I was an established sharpshooter with a keen eye for precision in stressful situations and was on constant call to travel on missions with other well-accomplished sharpshooters. I recalled being on several missions with the late assistant commissioner of police, Mr. Lawrence Major, on a fixed-wing aircraft, checking the Exuma Cays and the west side of Andros. On one occasion, we were directed to check on some unusual activities on Cay Sal. The civilian pilot of our aircraft was advised by Mr. Major that he was off course during our travel. The pilot disagreed. Moments later, as we exited the clouds, the mountains of Cuba became quite visible. Mr. Major asked him to take a sharp right turn and get out of Cuban airspace. He also warned us to prepare ourselves for Cuban MiG fighter aircraft escorting us to Cuba or for being shot out of the skies. This was before the sinking of The Bahamas' Defence Force vessel, the HMBS Flamingo. I knew I had a praying mother in Abaco to add to my own prayers; a calm spirit came over me. Mr. Major gave the pilot the coordinates that took us directly to Cay Sal.

I enjoyed working with Mr. Major. It was always an educational experience. He was an officer who had great wisdom and vision. This man would tell you stories of his experiences that would make the time pass by quickly. I truly believe we would not have made it back to our homes had he not been on that mission with us. He undoubtedly may have saved our lives. On another mission, we spent a night at the airport of one of the Exuma cays after receiving tips that an aircraft was coming in with narcotics. The drug trade saw so many Bahamians' lives foolishly snuffed away. I don't know whether they realized the danger involved or if they were blinded by the money involved. I often wondered if the risk, the family pain, and suffering were really worth it. Mr. Major was given a well-deserved honor posthumously by the Bahamian government, by naming one of the Royal Bahamas Defence Force crafts in his honor; well-deserved.

One of my team's missions took us to a cay on the west side of Andros, where two Androsians were gunned down. We were left on the cay to wait for a larger boat to carry the bales of suspected marijuana. We had no communication and spent a few nights there before we were picked up. It was the norm for us to be dropped off on cays and airstrips by helicopter and fixed-wing aircraft with cheese and crackers and the clothes on our backs. These trips could last for days. On this mission on the west side of Andros, one of the officers suffered a panic attack. That early morning, we heard the sound of a boat nearby and noticed that it was headed directly toward us. We took up safe positions with our firearms. All of a sudden, the officer moved from his position and ran into the line of fire in front of us, holding his head and screaming. We beckoned passionately for him to get down. Someone rushed to him and pulled him out of the way. Thank God it was our team that arrived to collect us and the drugs. That officer quit at the end of his contract.

Andros was a busy area for narcotic trafficking. One time again on the west side of Andros, we were there on a mission when we spotted a luxury yacht heading north that appeared to be heavily laden. Several senior persons were with us, including ASP Wilmore Dames and C/Inspector Vernon Wilkerson. Efforts were made to stop the yacht, with its waterline well below the water surface. Shots were exchanged. The vessel turned west in the direction of Cuba, failing to stop. The occupants hid themselves. After a good chase, the decision was made to discontinue and not risk entering Cuban waters.

In another incident, three members of my unit received an assignment to travel to Andros on a Cessna aircraft in the late 70s. We had information about some unusual activities on the west side of the island. An inspector accompanied us to lead the operation. After landing, we got a volunteer guide with his boat and proceeded to Williams Island on the northwest side of Andros. On the island, we were able to effect the arrest of three

Colombian nationals with a large quantity of dangerous drugs. On our way back to the mainland, which took most of the night, the inspector decided to enjoy the alcoholic beverages that the prisoners had on the boat. Eventually, he became incoherent and very drunk and fell asleep. We managed to secure both the inspector and the prisoners and kept watch throughout the night.

Haiti Visits

Our mission took me to Port-au-Prince, Haiti, three times on deportation trips involving illegal immigration. Our travel was on the MV East Store and the MV Lady Moore, government tenders. These trips had me in deep thought; I wondered why someone would cross the Atlantic Ocean on such small crafts with so many people. The risk of one's life must be the ultimate sacrifice for whatever their reasons are. I wondered how many souls have been lost seeking economic freedom. On one of our trips to Haiti, with over three hundred people, we experienced a horrendous voyage. The ocean let its fury out on us. We were on the MV Lady Moore. I realized that the ocean can be so peaceful and calm sometimes, and the next minute it can be so treacherous. The boat lost both engines. By all indications, it appeared that we were doomed to the ocean grave. Everything seemed to be over for us as waves crashed over our boat. The captain had no control. We were at the mercy of God. As the waves rolled over us, we held on for dear life. We were like a piece of rag in the open ocean waters. It felt like hours before the engines started again and the captain was able to regain a little control.

I noticed on three of my trips to Haiti, upon our arrival at the dock in Port-au-Prince, the deportees were always very quiet. One officer would come to the boat and collect up to three hundred persons. They would form two lines and the officer would escort them off the dock. My prayers go out to the people of Haiti for a better future.

Mission Tragedies

I lost a very good friend, Corporal 644 Autrey Jones, in an Operation Bahamas and Turks and Caicos (OPBAT) helicopter crash. I could have easily been on that mission. He and retired Supt. Tyrone Burrows were also top shooters in our unit. We became close friends and because we knew each other so well and could depend on one another in any situation, we went through several defensive operational scenarios. We had similar passions. Our assignments and duties were taken seriously by us.

Another colleague, Officer "Shoes" Poitier, was shot while on an operation at the airport on Bimini. When I spoke with him at Princess Margaret Hospital, he described the horrific experience he went through. The shooter approached him while he acted as though he was dead and held the gun to his head when the other accomplice called him away, saying that he was already dead. He believed that covering himself with his blood saved him.

Gifted Unselfish Officers

I was transferred to Criminal Records in 1980. The majority of my later years were spent in the Criminal Records Office as Forensic Crime Scene Specialist and Fingerprint Technician. The Magistrate and Supreme Courts in the Commonwealth of The Bahamas later recognized me as a fingerprint expert. I was trained locally by some of the most brilliant minds in forensic law enforcement: Mr. Kendal Lightbourne, Mr. McDonald Chase, Mr. Glinton Fernander, and the walking Professor, Mr. Wellington Francis. These gentlemen poured their hearts into instructing and advising us on fingerprint technology, crime scene investigations, policing and court procedures, the law, and its practice. I was well prepared in these disciplines, whether on a crime scene, at international courses, or during court presentations in The Bahamas or the Turks and Caicos Islands. Thanks to these gentlemen, my commitment to service was solidified. Mr. Francis spoke on my behalf at my wedding in

1981. He became a very good friend and confidant. I am always fascinated by his knowledge of the law, its practice, and politics. To this day, I look to him for sound advice and guidance.

The police criminal investigator I respected most was Detective Douglas Hanna. Mind you, there were some very dynamic Criminal Investigation Department (CID) investigators. I believe they all agree with my opinion of Mr. Hanna. I worked on several high-profile cases with him. He was meticulous and left no stone unturned. He had a passion for his craft and performed at a brilliant level. His presentation in court told the story. I remember him coming into the Criminal Records Office seeking information to put his cases together. He respected the crime scene investigators and worked with them to piece together the puzzle in order to either clear the accused or strengthen the case against them. I worked with him on the island of Abaco. There, he proved his character to me and gained my respect as an officer and a gentleman. He was never pompous, arrogant, or braggadocious about his abilities. You watched the man in action and knew he was a special breed when it came to investigations.

The Field Marshal and all-around ground police officer I worked with was Mr. Raymond Mackey. He was a fearless warrior with whom I went on many very dangerous missions, accompanied by Sergeant 923 John Rolle, in Abaco and its cays. We sometimes rode the entire island on the Abaco Highway, from Marsh Harbour to Sandy Point and on to Crown Haven. This was done sometimes twice a day despite horrible road conditions. On one of our regular patrols in North Abaco, we came across a drug transaction. A truck had just completed offloading suspected bales of drugs onto a go-fast boat. Everyone, including the truck owner, got onto the powerboat and sped off. We commandeered a small boat despite the owner's disapproval. It was late in the evening and the sun was setting in the west. The go-fast boat, with four engines attached to the stern, was stationary near a small cay, waiting for someone to collect the truck owner who was a local Abaconian. As we approached the go-fast boat, I noticed about five people onboard. When they recognized that we were there for a different reason, gunshots rang out! We were involved in a battle on the seas. During the exchange, the boat made a sharp turn and headed west at a very high rate of speed. We received information later that the truck owner was dropped off on the island of Grand Bahama and that one of the occupants on the boat was wounded.

Abaco, because of its vast land mass, major highways, several hundred acres of cane fields with spaces to accommodate large aircraft, seven airports, and close proximity to the United States of America, was an unlimited haven for drug trafficking. Sleep was a luxury for us! We worked fearlessly, tirelessly, and with dedicated commitment to our sworn profession—rain, sunshine, the very cold nights in the pine forest of Abaco, air patrol, sea patrol, and the many daily road trips covering hundreds of miles almost daily. Sometimes I wondered if the authorities were serious about fighting this scourge. They received daily reports in Nassau. However, nothing was done to help the situation. Manpower, equipment, and vehicles were not a priority for them to send to assist in the fight against drug trafficking. When boats and other crime-fighting equipment were part of an arrest, there was always an urgency to send them to Nassau. The boats and equipment were sold back to the drug dealers by the authorities in Nassau. It was a vexing problem, as the same boats were seen and searched within a few days back in Abaco.

I recall us using a particular aircraft operator to take us out in search of illegal operations, with emphasis on dangerous drug smuggling. The pilot was a heart patient with reportedly three heart operations under his belt. None of us knew how to fly a plane. After the second time on this aircraft, I was seriously contemplating taking up flying lessons. I thought it was important that I learned how to land an aircraft safely.

On another occasion, we were on our way back from court in Nassau on a police-chartered plane, piloted by someone whom I found out later was a student pilot. The young man came in for landing and was too high over the runway to make a decent landing. He made a sudden descent so as not to overshoot the runway. The experience was horrible. Sadly, he died in a plane crash several months later. At the time, he was the only occupant.

Often, we forget the female officers who contributed so much to the Royal Bahamas Police Force. Dorothy Davis was instrumental in my training at the Police College. She was a confident lady who stood out amongst the men and her peers. She was an outspoken, intelligent Officer. Delmetha Black Turnquest, a fingerprint expert, had a natural knack for dealing with criminal files and ensuring that the criminal identities were always up to date. Agatha Rodgers was a Security Intelligence Branch (SIB) Officer with a brilliant mind, focused with a no-nonsense attitude. Because of her intervention, several well deserving officers were awarded the Long Service and Good Conduct Medal. I have great admiration and respect for Juanita Colebrooke. I never worked directly with her. However, watching from a distance and seeing her in action, I could tell she was an officer par excellence, knowledgeable in her duties.

Impactful Crime Scenes

There are some things on my law enforcement journey that will always have a lasting impact on my life. I was deeply touched when I processed a scene where a young mother had drowned her two children. They were stuffed head down in five-gallon buckets near the downtown Nassau. I had children around the same age at that time. This was like a nightmare. That scene stayed with me for a very long time.

There was another scene where a culprit slit the throat of a six-year-old girl and raped her afterward, in the southwest area of New Providence. He was found a short time later and subsequently charged. The evil that men do is mind shattering.

Also, I processed a scene at a popular church and school office in the Over-the-Hill area of New Providence where a young lady had slit the throat of a respected religious figure to cover up her misappropriation of church finances. The victim had discovered a financial discrepancy. Eventually, the suspect was arrested, charged, and sentenced to prison. Detective Douglas Hanna was the chief investigator in this case.

I supervised a crime scene where a young man's throat was cut several times, ear to ear. This went beyond the norm, savagely done. I felt the pain of the father who identified the body at the Rand Laboratory, Princess Margaret Hospital (PMH). The very first time I saw a father passionately kiss his son in death while bitterly crying, my heart bled for him! I still see that outpouring of love to this day. That night, I went into the bedroom of my sons; they were peacefully sleeping. I thought of all my children and cried in silence, praying.

The senseless murder of a well-loved Anglican priest was heartbreaking, to say the least. This priest was the epitome of a

Investigating a crime scene (W. Bootle center)

selfless, Christ-like human being. He was killed by someone he trusted. What goes through the hearts of men? Only God has the answer!

Head of State Assignment

In early 1978, some of our unit members traveled to Grand Bahama after being detailed to work at the Conference of Heads of Government of the Caribbean Community (CARICOM) held in Freeport. I was assigned to Deputy Prime Minister of Jamaica, Mr. P. J. Patterson. He later served as prime minister of Jamaica. Mr. Patterson exhibited a quiet demeanor, a great personality, and didn't care much for the fanfare and attention. The conference chairman was Sir Lynden Pindling, Prime Minister of the Commonwealth of The Bahamas.

Shah of Iran

The highest profile and most menacing situation my team was involved in was the protection of the former Shah of Iran. Shah Mohammad Reza Pahlavi arrived in The Bahamas in March 1979. I was on the duty detail for the deposed monarch at the Ocean Club, Paradise Island. He was overthrown by the Iranian people after ruling for many years. Shortly afterward, the Iranian monarchy was formally abolished. The architect of the Iranian Revolution was Ruhollah Ayatollah Khomeini. He declared Iran an Islamic Republic, becoming the religious leader who took control of Iran. We were often briefed on the high risk of our duties because of the circumstances surrounding his overthrow. We received intel that an assassin squad was planning an assault on the location. However, it was not easy for them to get into the country.

His wife took walks along the sandy beach at night for long periods, accompanied by her personal security detail. We all received a signed letter from the Shah, thanking us for our service at the end of his family's stay.

President of Nicaragua

Anastasio Somoza, former president of Nicaragua, left office after insurgents led by the Sandinista National Liberation Front closed in on Managua. We were briefed to be on standby to travel wherever in The Bahamas President Somoza was going. We were to assist with his security detail. Later, we were advised that the risk was much too high for this assignment. Therefore, the mission was canceled. The easy access to The Bahamas from Nicaragua was undoubtedly a challenge to security. Somoza was assassinated in September 1980 while in exile in Paraguay.

Grand Bahama Young Men Disappearance

Panic shocked the island of Grand Bahama. Young boys went missing without a trace. Parents guarded and protected their children as this horrific mystery changed the lifestyle of the community. The thought of having a deranged killer in their midst was terrifying.

There were several notable cases that came under my remit as Crime Scene Director. The most known, perhaps, was this one in 2003. I was transferred to the Grand Bahama District and directed to lead a team of well-trained forensic crime scene investigators from New Providence and Grand Bahama in the investigation of five missing young boys and one young adult male in Grand Bahama.

We examined the residence of the children using all resources available to us. The examiners worked tirelessly during their examinations, leaving no area untouched. The unexplained sudden disappearing of these young boys had the community in a state of panic and fear. Parents and loved ones of these young boys were desperately seeking answers. Other parents were terrorized with the thought of having their children out of their sight. The forensic crime scene investigators were mandated to ensure that we looked at every piece of evidence with a fine-tooth comb and sharp eyes. We worked alongside our local and international forensic pathologists, an American forensic anthropologist, several international agencies, as well as local and international forensic personnel. I travelled with members of our forensic laboratory team to the forensic labs in Fort Lauderdale and Miami, Florida, with evidence to be examined. Many man-hours went into the processing of these crime scenes, meticulously and methodically examining several locations, inclusive of the forest, apartment buildings, homes, vehicles, personnel, and all areas of interest. The accused in these matters was arrested, tried, and subsequently sentenced to Her Majesty's Prison (HMP) to serve time.

Unsung Heroes

I am grateful for the men and women whom I had the opportunity to lead. I am indebted to them for making work an educational experience while standing together as a family unit.

Through the years, I worked with some outstanding crime scene officers in New Providence and Grand Bahama. They worked tirelessly to ensure that their work could stand up to scrutiny and ethically avoid bias, presenting evidence as it was found. They worked double and triple shifts with me, coming out to assist at crime scenes when they should have been resting for their tour of duty.

Recommendations were sent forward for some sort of recognition for them. However, I was told on several occasions that it was expected they would do these things. I still have some of that correspondence. Their integrity was remarkable. One of the officers had an assignment to work on the American pop singer, Aaliyah Haughton's, case. She died in a plane crash at Marsh Harbour, Abaco, in 2001 after filming a music video on that island. The officer brought the negatives and photographs to me for safekeeping after he was offered a large sum of money from unscrupulous individuals trying to release the pictures to foreign media.

I had a stellar career as a law enforcement officer with the RBPF. My regrets are few, if any. And if I had the choice again, I would do it all over. My only hope now is that this new generation will have the passion to fight the scourge of crime without seeking personal reward as a priority. It is my sincerest prayer that the RBPF, as best as possible, invests in forensic crime scene investigators and criminal investigators so that we may truly bring cases to a close without a doubt and with successful conclusions (in favor of the plaintiff or the accused) that will hold up to scrutiny at the Privy Council level.

Chapter II
RECOMMENDATIONS

Crime remains a significant challenge in our country, and finding a solution is essential for our economic survival. Urgent and difficult decisions need to be made to ensure the nation's future. Criminals have become increasingly bold due to the lack of consequences for their actions, feeling too comfortable as they carry out offenses. This situation is detrimental to any law enforcement agency. When individuals can commit the most egregious crimes without fear of being identified, it creates a dangerous scenario. We must address this issue promptly to protect our citizens from harm that could devastate The Bahamas as we know it. Additionally, we cannot overlook the threat to our key industry: tourism. A reactive response is simply insufficient and unacceptable.

The Royal Bahamas Police Force was established in 1840, celebrating 184 years this fifty first year of our nation's independence. The Force has evolved over the years, using the same manual of the old colonial rulers. The evolution was very slow or, in many cases, non-existent. I was flabbergasted when I heard a former Head, in a general meeting, say that he loved the existing Police Act at that time and wouldn't change a thing. I was expecting a clear vision for the organization from someone whom I thought was a twenty-first-century leader.

In order for growth in the war on crime, a commissioner must have a clear vision and a mission that is highly focused with no distractions. The top cop must exercise the freedom guaranteed under the constitution to carry out his or her duties without fear of contradiction regarding decisions made. There should be absolutely no political interference, especially where the legal enforcement of the law is concerned. Maybe the time has come for an elected constitutional commissioner of police.

There must be a stringent policy on elevation and qualified candidates must be recognized in promotional exercises. One should have the aptitude and professional acumen to hold a senior position. There should be training and retraining of prospective candidates—identify future officers at an early stage and put them through rigorous tests, preparing them for the future. We are doing them and the country a disservice by elevating persons with no skills in planning and crime fighting.

After 184 years and fifty-one years of independence, a future commissioner of police and his/her top team should present a 5-year policing plan to the country after consultation with all stakeholders. Due to the ever-changing environment, amendments and adjustments should follow as necessary. The present policing annual report has been an excellent tool, informing us of statistics, past events, and duties. This will complement a five-year policing plan and provide comprehensive insight into the future targets to be accomplished. Every year, there should be a breakdown of the main goals set and the accomplishments achieved, both negative and positive, showing what is being done and already in place to improve the weakest areas of the report.

Family Islands

The Bahamas is an archipelago consisting of numerous inhabited islands. Over the years, many of these islands have transformed significantly. However, some Family Islands have lagged in implementing effective and efficient policing strategies. There seems to be no clear policing plan that takes into account the unique characteristics of each inhabited island.

For instance, in Abaco, it is currently impossible to provide an accurate count of the island's population.

Like most islands, there are many large communities where the police are negligent in their visits. The public is knowledgeable about the crimes that go unchallenged. Drugs, prostitution, illegal gambling, unlicensed bars, illegal immigration, illegal buildings, grocery and clothing stores, flea markets—all matters that should be a priority in a national policing plan; or we will face the well-planned destruction of our once Bahamian nation.

After fifty-one years as a nation, I believe we are now facing a crisis. It is imperative to make legal decisions. Each major island should have a dedicated special court to address the increasing number of unique challenges we are encountering. Law enforcement officers must urgently take action, citing or arresting individuals for these obvious violations of our laws. Failing to do so would mean letting down future generations of Bahamians and fostering a culture that contradicts our fundamental values.

For years, the concentration of policing focused too much on New Providence and, to a very lesser extent, Grand Bahama. The Family Islands, for some reason, do not receive their fair share. I must commend all the government administrations for supplying the Force with the equipment and manpower needed. However, are the Family Islands receiving their fair share?

Exuma and Eleuthera are two of the fastest-growing islands in The Bahamas and could receive more vehicles and manpower to assist with the growing crime problems. Like Abaco, they are experiencing some of the same challenges. Even though many officers graduate every year, the Family Islands continue to not get their fair share of officers. As an example, West End has been left out of the general policing plan, even though human trafficking is a major challenge in that area. Over the years, they have been miserably below policing standards. The ferry hub between Abaco and Grand Bahama at McLean's Town and

Crown Haven is a national port that needs additional attention. Several hundred passengers and private boaters use that area weekly. This area could use the service of a police or Defence Force boat on location full-time. The southern islands of The Bahamas, half a century later, are still relatively untouched, with apparently no urgent plans for progress. It's a haven for illegal immigration, illegal fishing, and the trafficking of dangerous drugs.

Family Island Recruitment

It is now time to focus in earnest on Family Island policing. Firstly, recruitment on each island of qualified locals. Secondly, after training, it is mandatory to return to that island and to serve for a period of five years before eligibility for transfer. Of course, there should be a proviso in the case of certain circumstances. Thirdly, the necessary resources, equipment, and tools to fight crimes on the Family Island should have its own dedicated budget.

New Providence Policing

I believe the one thing you don't want to hear when reporting a crime to the police is, "We don't have a vehicle or anyone to dispatch to your complaint!" Further, not having your matter dealt with for three to four days should be a thing of the past. I believe that strategic deployment can contribute to a smoother operation. Poor deployment contributes to the proliferation of crime.

Firstly, there needs to be a manpower audit, followed by an equipment audit and duties assignment in each district. Do we need thirteen policing divisions with two to three officers on duty and a transportation shortage? Or should we have ten divisions with more resources and manpower assigned to those divisions? The ten divisions will now have additional vehicles and manpower to carry out community duties with a quick response. The other three stations could now be used as emergency outposts by the Fire Department, Ambulance Department, Social Services, Urban Renewal, and any other agencies that can assist the communities in record time. This takes time. However, with planning and collaboration with other agencies, this could be achieved. Planning must first start with the community's needs. Meet with them and seek their partnership.

I don't understand why people were being told by the police that they had no vehicle to visit their complaints or no one to send—or that it took three days to visit a scene. New Providence is only 21x7 miles, with over nineteen police stations and divisions. This does not include the detective and other police departments, which number over sixty in New Providence. There is a police population of around four thousand plus. I take into account that many retire, are discharged, or are dismissed. There is also a recruitment system in place and a police training college on New Providence and Grand Bahama. I have given this an analytical assessment over the years and have come to the conclusion that deployment is very poor.

Effective Grid System

For quick response and effective policing, more emphasis should be placed on the Mobile Division. I would recommend a real grid patrol system on New Providence. If there is one officer per vehicle, the other vehicles on patrol would always be in close proximity. There will be a wider range of visibility for the drivers and the community. When faced with a situation, other vehicles on the grid would be able to respond immediately, showing force. Whenever there is a report of any kind in the patrol officer's grid, that car would be the first to respond and take the necessary notes. The station investigators should respond as soon as possible. This system would reduce crime in hot spot areas and improve response time exponentially in the community.

Twenty-First-Century Crime-Fighting Equipment

The Police Department should now take possession of a helicopter as crime-fighting equipment. This would help with policing in The Bahamas. This can be in partnership with the Immigration Department, Defence Force, Customs Department, or Health for critical emergency services, and other essential duties. We are in a hurricane belt zone; a chopper will be an ideal transportation method to respond after the passage of a hurricane. This will offer a twenty-first-century policing strategy that will provide advantages in fighting illegal immigration, narcotics trafficking, illegal firearms, human trafficking, illegal goods importation, poaching, and other nefarious crimes committed on the open seas. We are an archipelago nation. Stop it before it enters our mainland. The real question is: are there other ways to fight the war on crime?

Primary School Crime Education

It's essential for the police to develop a proactive plan for recruiting at the primary school level, especially since gangs are targeting these young minds. Law enforcement can really make a difference by collaborating closely with the Ministry of Education, the teachers' union, principals, and the Parent-Teachers Association (PTA). Introducing a primary school policing initiative could become an exciting part of the curriculum, helping educate children about crime and its consequences in a supportive way. Engaging parents in this program is also crucial; we can help them understand the impact of modern technology, both good and bad. Let's create after-school programs for at-risk primary school children and come up with a system to support them all the way through high school. The Defence Force and Police Force can play a vital role in making this program a success!

Recruitment

Building a successful law enforcement organization starts with having an effective recruitment program at its heart. It's essential to never compromise on the vetting process. The focus should always be on integrity, especially given the many challenges that come with the role. Every recruit should be ready to stand firm on their principles. While the profession sometimes exposes you to the darker sides of humanity, this does not define who you are. Recruits should approach the journey with a heart to serve their country and prepare for a fulfilling and rewarding career ahead!

Department Public Prosecution

This recommendation highlights the importance of having the Department of Public Prosecutions (DPP) take on the exclusive responsibility for prosecuting all criminal matters in the magistrates' courts of The Bahamas. By making this transition, we will align our prosecutorial practices with modern legal standards, reflecting a commitment to justice, fairness, and professionalism. Additionally, this change aligns The Bahamas with jurisdictions like the United Kingdom, which have chosen to move away from relying on police prosecutors, recognizing the limitations and potential conflicts that can arise from that practice.

Background

At present, police prosecutors have an important role in managing cases in the magistrates' courts in The Bahamas. Although they provide a quick and economical approach to prosecution, this system faces challenges, such as possible conflicts of interest, insufficient legal training, and a decline in public trust regarding the fairness of prosecutions.

In 1986, the United Kingdom ended the use of police prosecutors and created the Crown Prosecution Service (CPS).

This change aimed to ensure that all prosecutions are handled by legally trained professionals who operate independently from the investigative process. This model has set a standard for prosecutorial independence throughout the Commonwealth.

Justification for Change

Improving impartiality - Police prosecutors belong to the same organization that investigates crimes. This dual function often leads to a perceived and sometimes actual conflict of interest, which erodes public trust in the justice system. By transferring prosecutorial duties to the DPP, a distinct separation between investigation and prosecution is established, enhancing confidence in the fairness of the judicial process.

Reducing police workload - Allowing police to focus exclusively on investigations and enforcement enhances operational efficiency. Removing prosecutorial duties enables law enforcement to allocate resources toward solving and preventing crime, benefiting the broader community.

Implementation Strategy: Gradual Transition

Develop a phased plan in which the DPP's office gradually takes over responsibility for certain categories of cases in the magistrates' courts. Include a timeline for the complete transition, accompanied by regular reviews of the capacity-building process. Expand the DPP's office by hiring additional legal professionals and increasing salaries to match those at the Attorney General's office to handle the increased workload. The continued reliance on police prosecutors in The Bahamas is an outdated practice that hinders the development of a robust and independent justice system. Transitioning all prosecution responsibilities in the magistrates' courts to the office of the DPP will enhance impartiality, professionalize legal proceedings, and align The Bahamas with international best practices. This reform is essential for strengthening public confidence in the rule of law and ensuring that justice is administered fairly and effectively.

> "Service to the public is not a job—it's a calling. And that calling requires an unwavering commitment to integrity, accountability, and fairness."
>
> *Cathy Lanier*

Chapter 12
FINAL THOUGHTS

I recall the first time I walked through the gate on East Street in Nassau to begin my official duties. Eight years later, on a Sunday morning, while working a solo twelve-hour shift at the Criminal Records Office, I received urgent information from Detective Sergeant 127 Christopher Rahming of the Interpol Department, acting on the directive of Mr. Ormand Briggs, Chief Superintendent of Police for the Criminal Investigation Department (CID).

Mr. Briggs was very impressed with the detailed report I put together. He called me the next day after viewing my file and said he was shocked I was a constable. He then advised me that he wanted me to go to Abaco to establish a Fingerprint and Crime Scene Section at Marsh Harbour, Abaco. I was promoted to corporal on the next exercise and to sergeant on the second promotion exercise after that. Throughout my career, it was through the grace of God that my work spoke for me. No doubt, God uses others to see your value.

The Final Walk

On Friday, October 26, 2012, I left my office at the Complaints and Corruption Unit around 7:30 p.m. This stroll down the corridor on the top floor of the Gerald Bartlett Complex Police Headquarters in Freeport, Grand Bahama, marked a bittersweet final walk just a week after my scheduled retirement on October 20. I had extended my hours without pay to assist the department until a replacement was appointed. Holding my piggy bank filled with silver coins and paper change, I was astonished to discover it totaled more than a month and a half of my salary! Ironically, Gerald Bartlett, the commissioner, embodied humility. I clearly remember him frequently visiting the Criminal Records Office on East Street, where he would sit and request, "Please assist me with a Character Certificate." When he needed a photo, he'd seek help at the office. He engaged in genuine conversations with us, exemplifying true leadership without a hint of superiority.

Whilst walking the quiet corridor, no one in sight, no sound, only my footsteps, I thought of my journey. It turned out to be priceless, fascinating! Life's greatest joys are in the journey, but every journey has its crossroads, stop signs, bumps, and disappointments; we must look for the positive, the fuel that propels us forward.

My Record

I retired at the age of fifty-eight, quietly and without any regrets, without receiving a Discharge Certificate. I began my career as a teenager and took less than ten days of sick leave over four decades. I received one medal for Long Service and Good Conduct. I also worked three and a half years of unpaid overtime.

Throughout my journey, I discovered that quality and dedication to service are inherent traits. Validation from others isn't necessary; what truly matters is doing your best in the eyes of God and being true to your own conscience and country.

As we strive for genuine nationhood after fifty-one years of independence, the importance of law and order is as crucial as the contribution of my young squad during our inaugural independence celebrations. They are interconnected and complement one another. We must communicate this clearly to children and youth, community leaders, our business and civic sectors, and all Bahamians, including those involved in crime. Our future progress hinges on this awareness. Key values such as patriotism, service, discipline, adherence to the law, and love are essential for reclaiming our noble Bahamian journey. It is our duty to share the narratives of our identity, our challenges, and the promises we have made to uphold our sovereignty.

For my part, I have penned this short love letter to my country and its people, saying, "Happy fifty-first anniversary!" It was God's grace that brought us safely this far. By God's grace, we shall continue moving forward, upward, onward, and together.

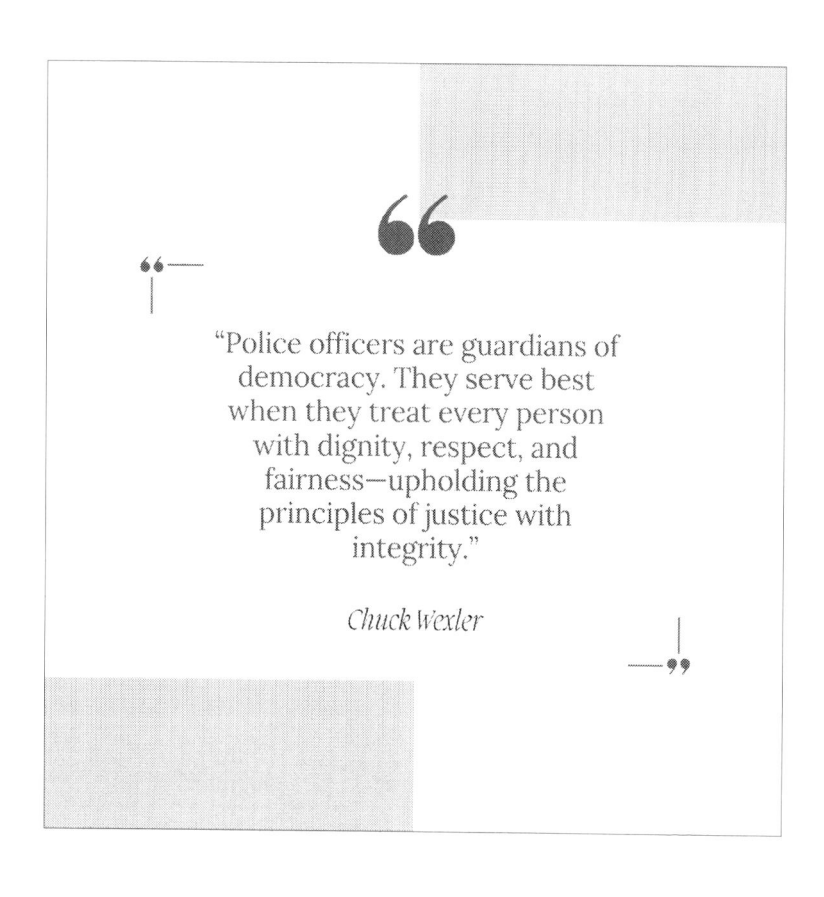

"Police officers are guardians of democracy. They serve best when they treat every person with dignity, respect, and fairness—upholding the principles of justice with integrity."

Chuck Wexler

Made in the USA
Columbia, SC
07 May 2025